DR. RAN
Plant-Based
VISIONARY
KITCHEN

Over 130 plant-based recipes for healthy vision

Notices & Disclaimers

Disclaimers / Legal Information

Notice of Liability

Trademark Notice

Copyright Information

A Message From Dr. Rani Banik

As an integrative ophthalmologist, I am a firm believer that food is medicine. What we put in our mouths can have a tremendous impact on the health of our visual system, as well as the entire body.

There is abundant scientific evidence that eye-smart nutrition can benefit common conditions such as dry eye, macular degeneration, cataracts, and glaucoma. Our eyes need a wide variety of nutrients – antioxidants, vitamins, minerals, amino acids, fats, and polyphenols to maintain healthy structure and optimal function.

I developed this plant-based recipe guide to help you support your eye health. Each recipe is carefully curated and designed to provide the critical nutrients necessary for healthy vision. Be sure to rotate through the various plant-based recipes in each category to provide your eyes with the full spectrum of nutrients needed.

Please keep in mind that his recipe book is intended to serve as an overall guide and is designed for a plant-based style of eating. If you have specific dietary needs or restrictions, please make adjustments and swap out foods or ingredients as necessary.

May these recipes be a feast for your eyes!

To your eye health,

Rani Banik, MD.

Table of Contents

Smoothies
&
Beverages

Smoothies & Beverages

almond cocoa smoothie

Makes 2 servings

Ingredients:

- 2 cups unsweetened almond milk
- 1 scoop vegan protein powder*
- 1 small avocado
- 1 tablespoon cocoa powder
- 1 teaspoon almond extract
- ½ cup ice cubes
- Stevia, to taste (optional)
- 1-2 cups loosely packed chopped kale
- almond slivers

Directions:

1. Put all ingredients in a blender in the order listed.
2. Blend all ingredients together in a blender starting on low speed and working up to high speed until smooth.
3. Add more or less ice to desired thickness.
4. Optional: top with almond slivers

Soy-free. Typical varieties include rice, pea, hemp. Should be sweetened with stevia or unsweetened altogether. 1 scoop should be ≈ 17g protein.

nectarine greens smoothie

Makes 1-2 servings

Ingredients:
- 2 cups sliced nectarines
- 1 cup kale
- 2 cups spinach
- 3 cups lettuce
- 1/2 tbsp cinnamon
- 1 scoop vanilla protein powder

Directions:
1. Add all ingredients together in blender and blend.

nectarine-cranberry smoothie

Makes 1-2 servings

Ingredients:
- 3 cups nectarine slice
- 1 1/2 cup cranberries
- 1 cup kale
- 2 cups spinach
- 1/2 tbsp cinnamon

Directions:
1. Add all ingredients together in blender and blend.

chocolate mint spinach smoothie

Makes 2 servings

Ingredients:

- 2 cups unsweetened almond or coconut milk
- 2 scoops vegan chocolate protein powder (pea, rice, or hemp)
- 3 cups baby spinach
- 1 teaspoon peppermint extract (or more, to taste)

Directions:

1. Put almond milk in a Vitamix or powerful blender.
2. Add protein powder, ice, and peppermint extract.
3. Add the baby spinach on top and start blender on low speed, and gradually work up to high speed for approximately 1 minute until smooth and well-blended.
4. Add more or less ice to desired consistency.

strawberry peach kale smoothie

Makes 2 servings

Ingredients:

- 2 cups unsweetened almond, hemp, or coconut milk
- 1 cup frozen strawberries (no sugar added)
- 1 cup frozen peaches (no sugar added)
- 2 cups fresh kale
- 1 teaspoon vanilla extract
- 2 scoops vanilla protein powder (pea, rice, organic soy, or hemp)
- Fresh basil (optional)

Directions:

1. Put all in a blender and mix well.
2. Add ice to make the smoothie slushier, if desired.
3. Top with fresh basil

Tips: Options include adding 1 tablespoon ground flax or chia seed to add omega-3 fats and/or substituting organic baby spinach for the kale.

multi-greens smoothie

Makes 2 servings

Ingredients:

- 1 cup kale, collard greens, or Swiss chard, packed tight (large stems removed)
- ½ cup loosely packed parsley leaves
- 1 medium apple, cored
- 1 medium pear, cored
- 1 tablespoon lemon juice
- 1 cup green tea, cold or room temp
- ½ cup water
- ¾ cup ice

Directions:

Put all ingredients in a high-power blender, and start on low speed, gradually working up to high speed for 1 minute.

Tips:

- This is best if served fresh, but it may be stored in the refrigerator to drink later in the day, if desired.
- Try to use a variety of different greens each time the Multi-Greens Smoothie is prepared if used daily or frequently during a focused detoxification period.
- If controlling carbohydrates more tightly, cut fruit portions in half.

strawberry-orange smoothie

Makes 1 serving

Ingredients:
- 1/2 cup strawberries
- 1/2 medium orange
- 3 cups chard
- 3 cups spinach
- 1/2 tbsp cinnamon
- 1 scoop vanilla protein powder

Directions:
1. Put together all ingredients in blender and blend.

mango-strawberry-greens smoothie

Makes 1 serving

Ingredients:
- 1/2 cup strawberries
- 2 cups of mango slice
- 3 cups chard
- 3 cups spinach
- 1/2 tbsp cinnamon
- 1 scoop vanilla protein powder

Directions:
1. Put together all ingredients in blender and blend.

rainbow smoothie

Makes 2 servings

Ingredients:
- ½ cup cold green tea
- 1 cup unsweetened hemp, coconut, or almond milk
- 2 tablespoons chia seeds, whole or ground
- ¼ teaspoon cinnamon
- ½ teaspoon fresh ginger, minced
- 1 tablespoon fresh lemon juice
- ½ cup frozen blueberries*
- ½ cup frozen strawberries*
- ½ cup frozen mango*
- ¼-½ cup ice to increase thickness, if desired (especially if using fresh fruit instead of frozen)
- 1 cup packed baby spinach

*No sugar added.

Directions:
1. Add prepared green tea, hemp, coconut, or almond milk to a blender. Then add the rest of the ingredients in the order listed, ending with baby spinach.
2. Blend at a very low speed until ingredients are mixed, then gradually increase speed to high, and blend well for 1 minute. Serve immediately.

Tips: If unable to serve immediately, omit chia or other seeds as gelling will occur and it be less palatable.
Optional: to provide more protein and healthy fats, add 1-2 scoops of vegan protein powder and 1-2 tablespoons nut butter, ground flax seeds, or hemp seeds.

chia berry mango smoothie

Makes 2 servings

Ingredients:

- 2 cups unsweetened almond, flax, hemp, or coconut milk
- 1 cup frozen strawberries or raspberries (no sugar added)
- 1 cup frozen mangoes (no sugar added)
- 2 scoops vanilla vegan protein powder*
- 2 tablespoons chia seeds
- Optional: 2 cups spinach leaves

Directions:

1. Add all ingredients to the blender and blend until smooth.

*Soy-free. Typical varieties include rice, pea, hemp. Should be sweetened with stevia or unsweetened altogether. 1 scoop should be ≈ 17g protein.

Tips: Use organic non-GMO soy milk for smoothie, if desired and if tolerated, to enhance detoxification.

chia berry coconut mango smoothie

Makes 2 servings

Ingredients:

- ½ cold green tea
- 1 cup full-fat canned unsweetened coconut milk
- 2 tbsps. chia seeds, whole or ground
- ¼ tsp cinnamon
- ½ tsp fresh ginger, minced
- 1 tbsp fresh lemon juice
- ⅓ cup frozen blueberries, no sugar added
- ⅓ cup frozen mango, no sugar added
- ¼-½ cup ice to increase thickness, if desired (especially use if using fresh fruit instead of frozen)
- 1 cup packed by baby spinach
- Stevia, to taste (optional)

Directions:

1. Add ingredients in the older listed (ending with baby spinach).
2. Blend at very low speed until ingredients are mixed, then gradually increase speed to high, and blend well for 1 min. Serve immediately.

Tip: If unable to serve immediately, omit chia or other seeds as they will gel and possibly make the smoothie less palatable for some.

raspberry greens smoothie

Makes 1-2 servings

Ingredients:

- 2 cups raspberries
- 3 cups arugula
- 3 cups kale
- 1/2 tbsp cinnamon
- 1 scoop vanilla vegan protein powder
- Optional: fresh mint leaves

Directions:
1. Put together all ingredients in a blender and blend.
Optional: top with fresh mint leaves.

multi-greens berry smoothie

Makes 2 servings

Ingredients:

- 1/2 cup strawberries or raspberries
- 2 cups of kale
- 3 cups chard
- 3 cups spinach
- 1/2 tbsp cinnamon

Directions:
1. Put together all ingredients in blender and blend.

cocoa kale smoothie

Makes 2 servings

Ingredients:

- 1 ½ cups unsweetened almond milk
- ½ cup full-fat canned unsweetened coconut milk
- 1 scoop protein powder
- 1 small avocado
- 1 tbsp cocoa powder
- 1 tsp almond extract
- ½ cup ice cubes
- Stevia, to taste (optional)
- 1-2 cups loosely packed chopped kale

Directions:

1. Put all ingredients in a blender in the order listed.
2. Blend all ingredients together in a blender, starting on low speed and working up to high speed until smooth.
3. Add ice and blend until you achieve desired thickness.

Tip: If unable to serve immediately, omit chia or other seeds as they will gel and possibly make the smoothie less palatable for some.

blackberry-greens smoothie

Makes 2 servings

Ingredients:

- 3 cups blackberries
- 2 cups kale
- 2 cups arugula
- 1/2 tbsp cinnamon
- 1 scoop vanilla vegan protein powder

Directions:
1. Put together all ingredients in blender and blend.

blackberry-apple smoothie

Makes 2 servings

Ingredients:

- 3 cups blackberries
- 2 cups apple slices
- 2 cups arugula
- 1/2 tbsp cinnamon

Directions:
1. Put together all ingredients in blender and blend.

cran-blueberry kale smoothie

Makes 1 serving

Ingredients:

- 1 cup unsweetened flax milk
- 1-2 scoops protein powder
- 1 tsp raw organic coconut butter
- ½ tbsp almond butter
- 2 cup kale, roughly chopped
- 1 cup organic berries (suggestion: ½ cup fresh or frozen cranberries + ½ cup fresh or frozen blueberries)

Directions:

1. Put ingredients in a blender in the order listed.
2. Blend on very low speed to start, gradually working up to high speed until well-blended.
3. Serve immediately for best results.

Tips:

1. Protein powders include pea or hemp.
2. Use frozen berries or add ice to make smoothie cold and of desired thickness.

citrus carrot juice spritzer

Makes 2 servings

Ingredients:
- 1 can (12 ounces) seltzer water
- 6 fluid ounces carrot juice
- 6 fluid ounces grapefruit juice
- 2 wedges of lime

Directions:
1. In a small pitcher, mix seltzer water and juices.
2. Fill 2 large glasses with crushed ice. Divide spritzer equally between the glasses.
3. Top with lime wedges.

kale pineapple banana smoothie

Makes 2 servings

Ingredients:
- 1 ½ cups unsweetened almond or coconut milk
- 1 cup chopped, packed kale
- ½ cup diced or chunk pineapple, fresh, frozen, or canned in juice and drained
- ½ banana (frozen is best)
- ½ cup ice, if desired
- 2 scoops vanilla protein powder
- 1 tablespoon chia or ground flax seed

Directions:
1. Add all ingredients to the blender and blend until smooth.

coconut milk

Makes 1 ⅔ cups (equivalent to one 13.5-oz can)

Ingredients:

- 2 cup organic coconut flakes (unsweetened)
- 2 ¾ cup water

Tips: The coconut milk will naturally separate after sitting in the fridge, so shake or blend well before using. Gently heating the milk will also help the coconut milk solids liquefy again. For a lighter milk alternative, combine 1.5 tbsps. coconut milk with about ¾ cup (6 oz) of water and blend in a blender until smooth.

Directions:

- In a saucepan over high heat, combine the coconut flakes and water. Bring to a full boil. Once water has reached a full boil, remove from heat, cover, and let sit for 1 hour.
- After 1 hour, pour the contents of the saucepan into a blender and blend on high for 2 to 5mins.
- Suspend a sieve or mesh strainer over a large mixing bowl and line the strainer with cheesecloth. Pour the blended coconut mixture into the lined strainer and let drain.
- Gather the edges of the cheesecloth together and squeeze the pulp, draining out the remaining milk into the bowl.
- Transfer the milk to a glass jar and store in the refrigerator or freezer.

almond milk

Makes 3 servings

Ingredients:

- ½ cup raw almonds
- 4 cup purified water
- 2 tablespoons pure natural sweetener (optional)
- Pinch of sea salt

Directions:

1. Soak almonds and 1 cup purified water in a blender, at room temperature, for about 6 hours.
2. After the almonds have soaked and using a strainer, drain off water and rinse well under running water.
3. Add almonds back to blender with 3 cups purified water, natural sweetener (optional), and sea salt. Blend on high for 2-3 minutes.
4. Strain with cheesecloth or strainer with fine holes, and pour into a container, squeezing out any remaining liquid.

Tips: The leftover almond pieces may be added to oatmeal or muffins or anything you can think of to benefit by adding lots of good fiber.

cranberry-peach smoothie

Makes 1 serving

Ingredients:

- 3/4 cup peach slices
- 1/2 cup cranberries
- 3 cups arugula
- 3 cups kale
- 1/2 tbsp cinnamon
- 1 scoop vanilla vegan protein powder

Directions:

1. Put together all ingredients in blender and blend.

peach-greens smoothie

Makes 1 serving

Ingredients:

- 4 cup peach slices
- 4 cups chard
- 3 cups lettuce
- 1/2 tbsp cinnamon
- 1 medium lemon

Directions:

1. Put together all ingredients in blender and blend.

make-ahead peppermint green tea

Makes 12 servings (1 serving = 1 cup/8 fluid ounces)

Ingredients:

- 12 cups water, divided
- 4 bags organic green tea
- 4 bags peppermint tea

Tip: Tea will stay fresh in the refrigerator for 5–7 days.

Directions:

1. Fill a glass coffee pot with 8 cups of water and add to coffee maker.
2. Place the 8 tea bags in the filter section of the coffee maker. Turn on coffee maker, and let it run through a cycle.
3. Pour the tea concentrate into a large pitcher, add 4 cups cool water, and serve.

Breakfast

Breakfast

apple cinnamon amaranth porridge

Makes 4 servings

Ingredients:

- 2 cups water
- 1 cup amaranth
- 1 large apple, skin on, cored, and diced
- ¼ teaspoon ground cinnamon
- ½ teaspoon sea salt
- optional toppings: walnuts or pecans

Directions:

1. In a medium saucepan, add all ingredients and bring to a boil. Stir frequently.
2. Reduce heat to low and simmer (covered) for 20-25 minutes until amaranth is soft
3. Top with nuts if desired..

Tips: Make the night before and reheat in the morning. Store leftovers in airtight glass container in refrigerator for up to 5 days. Serve with coconut or almond milk added to desired thickness.

overnight steel-cut oats

Makes 8 servings (1 serving = one level ¾ cup)

Ingredients:

- 6 cups water
- ½ teaspoon sea salt
- 1 ½ cups steel cut oats (gluten-free, if desired)

Directions:

1. Add water to saucepan and bring to a boil.
2. Add oats, cover and remove from heat. Place in refrigerator on a hot pad and leave overnight.
3. In the morning, reheat the oatmeal over low heat. (May need to add water to achieve desired consistency.)
4. Refrigerate what you don't eat.

Tips: Add modest portions of nuts, seeds, fruits, and spices, as desired.

chia pomegranate oatmeal

Makes 2 servings

Ingredients:

- 1 ⅓ cups water
- ⅔ cup rolled oats (old-fashioned)
- 1 pinch sea salt
- ½ teaspoon cinnamon
- 2 teaspoons chia seeds
- ½ cup pomegranate seeds

Directions:

1. Put water in a small saucepan and bring to boil. Add in rolled oats and pinch of salt.
2. Return to boil and reduce heat to simmer for 5 minutes. Rolled oats should thicken as they cook.
3. When ready to serve, stir in cinnamon, chia seeds and pomegranate seeds.

pumpkin oatmeal pancakes

Makes 4 servings

Ingredients:

- 1 cup plus 2 tablespoons gluten-free rolled oats
- 2 teaspoons cinnamon
- ¼ teaspoon nutmeg
- ¼ teaspoon ginger powder
- ¼ teaspoon cloves or allspice
- ½ teaspoon salt
- ½ teaspoon baking soda
- ⅔ cup pumpkin puree
- ⅓ cup unsweetened applesauce
- ⅓ cup unsweetened coconut beverage or almond milk
- 2 tablespoons coconut oil, melted
- 1 tablespoon natural sweetener
- 1 teaspoon vanilla extract

Egg replacer:

- ⅓ cup water
- 2 tablespoons ground flax seed

Directions:

1. Prepare the egg replacer by mixing the ground flax and water. Allow to sit for 5 minutes to gel.
2. Blend the oats in a high-speed blender until finely ground, about 60 seconds. Add the spices, salt, and baking soda.
3. In another bowl, whisk together the pumpkin, applesauce, milk, melted coconut oil, natural sweetener, vanilla, and egg replacer. Add the wet ingredients to the dry and stir until just combined. Do not over-mix.
4. Heat a non-stick pan or cast-iron skillet over medium heat (or 350 degrees F for an electric griddle). Lightly oil or butter the surface. Once the pan is hot, pour ¼ cup amounts of the batter, and gently spread the circles. Cook until bubbles form around the edges of the pancake.
5. These pancakes take slightly longer to cook than regular pancakes so just keep the heat on medium and give them some time. Flip and cook for another 2 minutes on the other side. Serve warm with a drizzle of organic agave nectar or natural sweetener.

vegetable tofu scramble

Makes 1 serving

Ingredients:

- 1-pound regular tofu, drained and crumbled
- 1 tablespoon water
- 1 teaspoon extra-virgin olive oil
- 1 cup assorted chopped raw vegetables (onions, red bell peppers, tomatoes, broccoli, zucchini, summer squash, asparagus, mushrooms, etc.)
- 1 pinch sea salt
- 1 pinch freshly ground black pepper
- 2 tablespoons chunky tomato salsa

Directions:

1. In a small cast iron pan, heat the oil over medium heat, and add the vegetables. Sauté until the vegetables are tender but still crisp (about 2-3 minutes).
2. Heat oil in a large skillet over medium heat. skillet to low heat and sauté tofu until dry, about 3 minutes. Add vegetables to tofu, scramble well, and cook until vegetables are heated through.
3. Season with sea salt and black pepper, and top with the salsa.

tofu sweet potato scramble

Makes 4 servings

Ingredients:

- 1-pound regular tofu, drained and crumbled
- 2 tablespoons low-sodium tamari
- 3 tablespoons olive oil
- ½ cup onion, chopped
- 1 medium sweet potato, diced
- ½ cup fresh crimini mushrooms, sliced
- ½ cup red or yellow bell pepper, chopped
- 1 clove garlic, minced
- ½ teaspoon thyme
- ¼ - ½ teaspoon red pepper flakes
- ½ teaspoon chervil or coriander
- 1 tomato, cut in wedges for garnish

Directions:

1. In a small bowl, stir tofu with tamari, and set aside.
2. Heat oil in a large skillet over medium heat. Sauté onions and sweet potatoes about 5 minutes until onions are translucent and potatoes are golden-brown.
3. Add mushrooms, bell pepper, garlic, and spices, and cook 3-5 minutes longer, until peppers and mushrooms are soft. Remove from heat, transferring vegetables to a bowl.
4. Return skillet to low heat and sauté tofu until dry, about 3 minutes. Add vegetables to tofu, scramble well, and cook until vegetables are heated through. Serve immediately, garnished with wedges of tomato.

hemp chia steel-cut oats in a jar

Makes 4 servings

Ingredients:

- 1 cup steel-cut oats
- 1 cup unsweetened hemp, almond, or coconut milk
- 2 tablespoons chia seeds
- ¼ teaspoon vanilla extract
- ¼ teaspoon ground cinnamon
- 1 pinch nutmeg
- 4 mason jars, with lids
- 4 tablespoons shredded coconut, optional
- 4 tablespoons chopped walnuts, pistachios, or berries, optional

Directions:

1. In a medium bowl, combine oats, milk, chia seeds, vanilla, cinnamon, and nutmeg, and stir to combine well. Divide evenly between 4 mason jars. Cover and refrigerate overnight.
2. Remove from refrigerator, when ready to eat, or if you prefer, allow to come to room temperature before eating. Add 1 tablespoon each of coconut and nuts per serving.

granola

Makes 8 servings (1 serving = ½ cup)

Ingredients:

- ½ cup cashews, soaked for 8 hours
- ½ cup pecans, soaked for 8 hours
- ½ cup sunflower seeds, soaked for 8 hours
- ½ cup pumpkin seeds, soaked for 8 hours
- 1 cup blueberries, fresh or frozen
- 2 tbsps. ground cinnamon
- 1 tsp vanilla extract
- ½ tsp nutmeg
- ½ tsp sea salt
- ½ cup organic dried coconut flakes (unsweetened)
- ¼ cup unrefined, organic coconut oil

Directions:

- Drain and rinse cashews, pecans, sunflower and pumpkin seeds after soaking. Place on a towel and lightly pat dry.
- Puree blueberries in a food processor until smooth.
- Add nuts, seeds, blueberry puree, and remaining ingredients to the food processor. Pulse to form a chunky paste.
- Prepare a food dehydrator with nonstick drying sheet or parchment paper. Spread mixture evenly on drying racks.
- Dehydrate for 12-24 hours at 145 degrees F, stirring once or twice.
- Break up the granola and store in an airtight container in the fridge.

Tips: If you do not have a dehydrator, you can use the oven Spread the mixture on a cookie sheet and bake at the lowest oven setting for 12-24 hours. Watch closely to avoid burning.

nut porridge

Makes 2 servings

Ingredients:

- 2 tbsps. dried coconut flakes (unsweetened)
- 2 tbsps. pumpkin seeds
- 2 tbsps. ground flax seeds
- 2 tbsps. chia seeds
- ¼ cup raw walnuts ½ tsp ground cinnamon
- ⅛ tsp sea salt
- 1 cup boiling water

Directions:

- Combine all dry ingredients in a high-speed blender and blend until finely ground.
- Pour boiling water into blender, cover with lid, and blend. Start on low setting and gradually move to high. Blend until porridge is smooth.
- Transfer porridge to a bowl and garnish with organic berries.

Tip: Soak the nuts and seeds for 8-12 hours or overnight (be sure to drain and rinse well) to improve digestibility. Make sure nuts and seeds are dry before blending in blender.

Salads
&
Sides

Salads and Sides

Salads and Sides

kale salad

Makes 6 servings (1 serving ≈ 1 cup)

Ingredients:

- 1 bunch kale
- ½ teaspoon sea salt
- ¼ cup diced red onion
- ⅓ cup currants, raisins, dried cranberries, pomegranate, or cherries
- ⅓ cup sliced apple (about ½ an apple)
- ⅓ cup sunflower seeds, toasted
- ¼ cup olive oil
- 2 teaspoons red wine vinegar or unfiltered apple cider vinegar
- Optional- pecans or walnuts

Directions:

- De-stem kale by pulling leaves away from stems. Wash leaves, spin, or pat dry. Stack leaves roll up and cut into thin ribbons. Put kale in a large mixing bowl.
- Add salt and massage it into the kale with your hands for 2 minutes (skipping this step will leave you with tough, stringy kale).
- Stir onions with fruit, apple, and sunflower seeds into the kale. Dress with oil and vinegar.
- Taste for sea salt and vinegar, adding more if necessary. Also taste a few bites to see if balance of sweet/sour/crunch/chewy are all well mixed. Add extra of what you miss.

purple cabbage salad

Makes 6 servings (1 serving ≈ 1 cup)

Ingredients:

- 1 small head of purple cabbage
- 3 carrots, shredded
- 1 tablespoon balsamic vinegar
- 1 ½ tablespoons unseasoned rice vinegar
- 1 tablespoon water
- ¼ teaspoon sea salt
- ¼ teaspoon pepper
- 1 tablespoon olive oil
- Optional:
- ¼ cup slivered almonds
- 1 cup pink grapefruit sections, cut in half

Directions:

1. Core the cabbage, and process through the slicing disc of a food processor (or slice thinly to make strips). Shred carrots by hand or food processor. In a large bowl, toss together cabbage and carrots.
2. In a small bowl, whisk together both vinegars, water, sea salt and pepper. Slowly drizzle the oil in while whisking to emulsify. Pour over cabbage and carrots, and toss. Allow dressing to marinate salad for 30-60 minutes before serving.
3. Just before serving, toss the cabbage mixture with the almonds and grapefruit sections.

roasted root vegetable salad

Makes 4 servings

Ingredients:

- 1 medium sweet potato (about 4 oz), cut into ¾-inch cubes
- 1 medium yellow potato, cut into ¾-inch cubes (may substitute parsnip)
- 1 medium carrot, peeled, cut into ¾-inch slices
- 1 small red onion, cut into ½-inch wedges
- 2 medium celery stalks, cut into ¾-inch slices
- 1 medium beet, cut into ¾-inch cubes
- 1 ½ tablespoons extra virgin olive oil, divided
- ¼ teaspoon sea salt
- ¼ teaspoon freshly ground black pepper
- 1 teaspoon balsamic vinegar
- 2 teaspoons fresh lemon juice
- ½ teaspoon Dijon mustard
- 1 tablespoon fresh parsley, chopped
- 1 teaspoon fresh cilantro, chopped
- 2 tablespoons walnuts, finely chopped

Directions:
- Preheat oven to 425 degrees F.
- In a large bowl, toss together potatoes (sweet and yellow), carrot, red onion, celery, beet, and ½ tablespoon of the oil, coating well. Season with sea salt and pepper.
- Arrange vegetables on a cookie sheet and spread mixture evenly in a single layer. Roast, stirring several times, until tender and beginning to brown, about 50 minutes.
- In a small bowl, whisk together vinegar, lemon juice, and Dijon mustard with remaining 1 tablespoon oil, and stir in parsley and cilantro. Drizzle dressing over vegetables, add walnuts, and gently toss.
- Serve warm or at room temperature.

asian salad

Makes 10 servings (1 serving ≈ ½ - ¾ cup)

Ingredients:

Salad:
- 1 medium head Napa cabbage, end cut off & cut into quarters
- 8 ounces bean sprouts
- 1 small jicama or daikon, peeled & sliced into thin pieces
- 1 bunch green onions, thinly sliced, dark green ends discarded
- 1 large red bell pepper, cut in half & sliced very thin
- 1 stalk celery, sliced very thin
- ½ cup slivered almonds
- 1 bunch cilantro, chopped (set aside several tablespoons for garnish)
- Optional: crispy wontons

Dressing:
- ⅔ cup grapeseed or olive oil
- ⅓ cup rice vinegar*
- 1 tablespoon sesame oil
- 3 tablespoons Dijon mustard
- 1 clove garlic, minced
- 3-inch piece fresh ginger
- 1 teaspoon agave syrup
- 2 pinches salt
- 2 pinches black pepper

*Be sure to use unseasoned rice vinegar (no sugar added).

Directions:

- Whisk all dressing ingredients together and set aside. This can be made up to several days ahead of time and stored in the refrigerator.
- Prepare the salad: A. Slice each quarter of cabbage very thin and place into a large serving bowl. B. Add bean sprouts, jicama, or daikon, green onion, pepper, and celery and mix well to combine.
- Add half the cilantro and half the dressing and toss well. Allow to sit for a few minutes to blend.
- Just prior to serving toss in almonds and garnish with remaining cilantro and wontons.

asparagus and kohlrabi salad

Makes 6 servings (1 serving ≈ 1 ⅔ cup arugula and ⅔ cup asparagus mixture)

Ingredients:

- 1 pint fresh organic strawberries (or 2 cups sliced)
- 1-pound asparagus ends discarded
- 2 medium Kohlrabi, peeled
- 2 tablespoons olive oil, divided
- ¼ pound arugula (or use ½ pound watercress)
- 1/2 cup strawberries
- 2 teaspoons balsamic vinegar
- 1 pinch salt
- 1 pinch black pepper

Directions:

1. Cut asparagus stalks into ¼- inch diagonal slices, separating tips. Prepare kohlrabi by slicing in ½-inch strips.
2. In a wok or large sauté pan, stir-fry asparagus stalks and kohlrabi in 1 tablespoon olive oil over medium heat until slightly browned. Add asparagus tips and continue to stir-fry for another 4-5 minutes. Remove from heat and toss with salt and pepper.
3. Pile arugula (or watercress) in a salad bowl and toss with remaining 1 tablespoon olive oil. Top with asparagus and kohlrabi. Add strawberries and and drizzle with balsamic vinegar. Serve immediately.

orange roasted beet arugula salad

Makes 4 servings

Ingredients:

- 2 large beets
- 1 navel orange
- 1 tablespoon olive oil
- 2 teaspoons balsamic vinegar
- 3 tablespoons orange juice
- 1 teaspoon Dijon mustard
- 1 pinch sea salt
- 1 pinch ground black pepper
- 2 bunches arugula, washed well and dried

Directions:

1. Preheat oven to 450 degrees F.
2. Wrap each beet in aluminum foil and place on a baking sheet. Roast for 40-50 minutes. Pierce with the tip of a sharp knife to test for tenderness. Remove from oven; when cool enough to handle, rub off skins. Slice into chunks.
3. While beets are roasting, slice off ends of orange with a sharp knife. Peel and break into segments. Cut each segment into 2-3 pieces. Set aside.
4. Once beets have cooled, whisk together olive oil, balsamic vinegar, orange juice, Dijon mustard, sea salt and black pepper.
5. In a large bowl, add arugula and toss with dressing. Add beets and oranges and toss again. Serve immediately.

spring vegetable salad

Makes 8 servings (1 serving = ½ cup)

Ingredients:

- 2 ½ tbsps. fresh lemon juice
- 3 tbsps. extra-virgin olive oil
- 1 clove garlic, crushed
- ½ tsp sea salt
- ½ tsp black pepper
- 1 lb. asparagus
- 1 cup fresh or frozen peas
- ½ English cucumber, cut into fourths and sliced (unpeeled)
- 3 scallions, sliced, white part only
- 1 ripe avocado, diced in 1-inch cubes

Directions:

Combine lemon juice, oil, garlic, salt, and pepper in a jar and shake vigorously. Set aside.

1. Snap ends off asparagus and slice 1-inch pieces diagonally. Blanch for 3 mins in boiling water, pour into strainer, and run under cold water.
2. Combine veggies in a bowl. Shake dressing and toss into salad. Add avocado right before serving.

Tips: For a variation, try raspberries in place of strawberries, and sliced almonds in place of walnuts.

caesar salad

Makes 4 servings

Ingredients:

Salad
- 24 romaine lettuce leaves (approximately 3 romaine hearts)

Dressing:
- 2 cloves garlic, finely minced
- 1 ½ tsp Dijon mustard
- 2 tbsps. tahini
- Juice from half a lemon (approximately 1 ½ tbsps.)
- 2 tbsps apple cider vinegar
- 2 tbsps. extra-virgin olive oil
- 1 pinch sea salt
- 1 pinch black pepper
- Optional: croutons

Directions:

1. Prepare the dressing by placing all dressing ingredients in a blender and processing until smooth (about 1 min, or until desired consistency is reached).
2. Wash, dry, and tear the lettuce into bite-size pieces with your hands. Place in a large salad bowl.
3. Add dressing and toss to coat. Top with croutons and season with extra black pepper if desired.

fruity spinach salad

Makes 4 servings

Ingredients:

- 1-pint fresh organic strawberries (or 2 cups sliced)
- 8 oz. fresh spinach, washed, dried, torn to pieces

Dressing:
- 1 tablespoon sesame seeds
- ½ tablespoon poppy seeds
- 1 scallion, chopped
- 1 tablespoon flax seed oil
- 1 tablespoon olive oil
- 2 tablespoons balsamic vinegar

Garnish:
- ¼ cup chopped walnuts

Directions:

1. Cut berries in half and arrange over spinach in serving bowl.
2. Combine dressing ingredients in blender or food processor and process until smooth. Just before serving, pour over salad and toss.
3. Garnish with nuts.

Tips: For a variation, try raspberries in place of strawberries, and sliced almonds in place of walnuts.

lemon avocado salad

Makes 2 servings

Ingredients:

- 4 cup arugula and mixed spring greens
- 1 green onion, chopped
- ¼ avocado
- 2 tbsps. balsamic vinegar
- 2 tsps. fresh lemon juice
- 1 pinch sea salt
- 1 pinch black pepper
- 2 tbsps. extra-virgin olive oil
- Optional: pomegranate arils or diced green apple

Directions:

1. Place greens and green onion in a medium bowl.
2. For the creamy avocado vinaigrette: in a small food processor, combine the avocado, vinegar, lemon juice, salt, and pepper. Blend until mixture is smooth and creamy. With processor running on low, drizzle olive oil through the opening until just combined.
3. Toss the vinaigrette with the greens and serve.

lemon cashew kale salad

Makes 4 servings

Ingredients:

- 1 tbsp extra virgin olive oil
- 1 tbsp lemon juice
- 1 pinch freshly ground black pepper
- 3-4 cups fresh kale, chopped ribbon style
- ¼ tsp sea salt
- ¼ cup raw cashews, finely chopped

Directions:

In a small bowl, whisk together olive oil, lemon juice, and black pepper. Set aside.

1. Place kale in a large bowl. Massage it by hand with sea salt for two mins until the kale is soft and dark green. (You may want to set a timer, as it is necessary to tenderize the kale for this long.) It will shrink quite a bit.
2. Add the olive oil mixture and the chopped cashews to the kale. Toss until the kale is evenly coated. Serve immediately.

Tips: Leftovers will keep well in the refrigerator for a day or two.

basic greens

Makes 6 servings (1 serving ≈ ½ cup)

Ingredients:

- 1 large bunch of kale, collards, or bok choy, washed
- 2-3 cloves garlic, minced or cut into slivers
- 1 tablespoon olive or coconut oil
- ½ cup vegetable broth

Variation: Season with dry chipotle pepper, balsamic vinegar, ground cumin or curry powder.

Directions:

1. Cut out the tough center stem from the kale or collards, chop, or slice into small pieces. Bok choy has no tough center so just chop into small pieces.
2. Sauté garlic in olive or coconut oil for about 30 seconds over medium heat. Add chopped greens and sauté for about 3-4 minutes.
3. Bok choy needs no further cooking. For kale or collards, add broth, cover, and simmer over low heat for about 10 minutes.

oven-roasted vegetables

Makes 4 servings

Ingredients:

- 1 cup broccoli florets
- 1 cup cauliflower florets
- 1 cup carrots
- 1 cup bell peppers
- 1 cup onion
- 1 cup mushroom
- 1 cup yellow squash
- 1 cup asparagus
- ¼ cup olive oil
- 1 tablespoon minced garlic
- ½ teaspoon salt
- ½ teaspoon ground black pepper

Directions:

1. Preheat oven to 375 degrees F while preparing vegetables. Chop vegetables so that all pieces are approximately the same size. This will ensure all vegetables are done cooking at the same time.
2. In a large roasting pan or cookie sheet, together all ingredients and spread in a single layer.
3. Roast approximately 25-30 minutes until veggies are tender and slightly brown, stirring occasionally.

Variation: For more seasoning, add dry chipotle pepper, balsamic vinegar, ground cumin, or curry powder.

sauteed sesame green beans

Makes 4 servings

Ingredients:

- 1-pound petite green beans, fresh or frozen
- 1 tablespoon extra-virgin olive oil
- 2 cloves garlic (or 2 teaspoons minced garlic)
- 1 tablespoon fresh basil (or 1 teaspoon dried)
- 1 tablespoon roasted sesame seeds
- 1 teaspoon unrefined sea salt
- ½ teaspoon pepper, or to taste

Directions:

1. Steam green beans in a steamer basket over water for 7-8 minutes. Once they are bright green and fork tender, remove from heat and drain. Set aside.
2. Heat a large skillet on medium. Add olive oil and garlic, and sauté for about 2-3 minutes. Garlic should be slightly browned but be careful not to burn.
3. Add steamed green beans to the pan, and sauté until green beans are warm and coated with olive oil and garlic.
4. Remove from heat. Immediately toss with basil, roasted sesame seeds, salt, and pepper. Serve warm.

Tip: This dish tastes great as a leftover.

simple roasted butternut squash

Makes 4 servings

Ingredients:

- 4 cups cubed butternut squash
- 2 tablespoons olive oil
- 2 cloves garlic, minced
- ¼ teaspoon salt
- ¼ teaspoon pepper
- Garnish: cilantro or parsley

Directions:

1. Preheat oven to 400 degrees F.
2. In a large bowl, toss together butternut squash, olive oil, garlic, salt, and pepper.
3. Pour coated squash on a baking sheet in a single layer.
4. Roast at 400 degrees F until squash is tender and lightly browned (about 25-30 minutes).
5. Garnish with cilantro or parsley.

yellow rice

Makes 8 servings (1 serving ≈1/2 cup)

Ingredients:

- 2 cups low-sodium vegetable broth
- 1 small onion, finely chopped
- 2 teaspoons olive oil
- 1 clove garlic, minced
- ½ teaspoon turmeric
- 1 up long-grain rice (brown, uncooked)

Directions:

1. In a 2-quart saucepan over low heat, sauté onions in oil until tender, about 5 minutes.
2. Add the garlic and sauté 1 minute.
3. Stir in turmeric, then rice. Add broth. Bring to a boil, cover, and simmer 45 minutes over low heat or until rice is tender and all liquid is absorbed. Do not stir.

balsamic roasted beets

Makes 2 servings

Ingredients:

- 1 bunch trimmed beets (about 4 beets)
- 1 tablespoon balsamic vinegar
- 2 pinches sea salt
- 2 pinches black pepper
- rosemary sprigs for garnish

Directions:

1. Preheat the oven to 400° F.
2. Gently scrub beets, and pat dry. Wrap in foil, and roast until tender (about 1 hour). Let cool, then peel and dice.
3. Place beets in a medium bowl, toss with balsamic vinegar, sea salt, and pepper, and serve.
4. Top with rosemary sprigs.

marinated vegetables

Makes 12 servings (1 serving ≈ ½ cup)

Ingredients:

- ¼ cup olive oil
- ¼ cup balsamic vinegar
- 1 teaspoon dried oregano
- 1 teaspoon dried basil
- 3 cloves garlic, cut into slivers
- ½ teaspoon sea salt
- 1 can (14 ounces) artichoke hearts, canned in water, cut into halves or quarters
- 1 can (14 ounces) hearts of palm, cut into ¼ -inch slices
- 1 can (6 ounces) pitted black olives
- ½ pound mushrooms, cleaned and quartered

Directions:

1. In a large bowl, whisk together olive oil, balsamic vinegar, oregano, basil, garlic, and sea salt.
2. Add artichokes, hearts of palm, olives, and mushrooms, and toss well.
3. Cover and place in refrigerator to marinate for 6 to 8 hours, tossing periodically.

Tips: Leftover marinade can be used as a salad dressing.

roasted Brussels sprouts

Makes 4 servings

Ingredients:

- 4 cups Brussels sprouts, cleaned and halved or quartered
- 2 cloves garlic, minced (about 2 teaspoons minced)
- 1 small apple, peeled, cored, and cut into eighths
- 1 tablespoon extra-virgin olive oil
- ¼ teaspoon sea salt
- ¼ teaspoon black pepper

Directions:

1. Preheat the oven to 375 degrees F.
2. In a large bowl, toss together all ingredients.
3. Pour out into a cookie sheet lined with parchment paper and spread mixture evenly in a single layer.
4. Roast uncovered for 20 minutes.

cooked red quinoa

Makes 8 servings (1 serving ≈ ½ cup)

Ingredients:

- 2 cups water
- 1 pinch sea salt
- 1 cup red quinoa, rinsed & drained

Directions:

1. Bring water to a boil in a medium heavy saucepan.
2. Add sea salt and quinoa. Cover, and bring to a boil. Reduce heat to low, and simmer for 12 to 15 minutes.
3. Remove from heat, and let sit, covered, for 5 more minutes before serving.

Tips: Garnish with chopped fresh chives or basil, if desired.

roasted cauliflower with pine nuts

Makes 6 servings (1 serving ≈ ½ cup)

Ingredients:

- 1 head cauliflower, broken into florets
- 2 cloves of garlic, peeled and minced
- 2 tablespoons extra virgin olive oil
- 1 teaspoon fresh rosemary, finely chopped
- ½ cup raw pine nuts
- ¼ teaspoon sea salt
- ¼ teaspoon freshly ground pepper

Directions:

1. Preheat oven to 425 degrees F. Place cauliflower florets in a large mixing bowl. Add garlic and stir thoroughly. Pour in olive oil and ensure that all cauliflower pieces are coated with oil. Sprinkle with rosemary, pine nuts, salt, and pepper.
2. Transfer mixture evenly onto baking sheet, being sure that mixture is spread evenly in a single layer.
3. Roast, uncovered, for 20-25 minutes or until the top and edges of cauliflower are lightly brown. You may stir about halfway through if they are becoming too brown. Serve immediately.

rosemary roasted potatoes

Makes 8 servings (1 serving ≈ ½ - ¾ cup)

Ingredients:

- 3 tablespoons olive oil
- 3-4 tablespoons chopped fresh rosemary
- ½ teaspoon garlic powder
- ¼ teaspoon sea salt
- ¼ teaspoon black pepper
- 2 pounds new potatoes, cut in half or fourths (red skin, purple, Yukon Gold, fingerling)

Directions:

1. Preheat the oven to 425 degrees F.
2. Stir together oil, rosemary, garlic powder, sea salt, and pepper in a large bowl.
3. Add potatoes and toss well until coated.
4. Spread evenly in a 15 x 10-inch baking pan.
5. Bake uncovered, for 30-35 minutes, occasionally stirring until potatoes are fork-tender and golden brown.

sauteed baby bok choy

Makes 4 servings

Ingredients:

- ½ cup mirin
- 1 tablespoon low-sodium tamari
- 4 heads baby bok choy (1 ¼ pounds total), halved lengthwise

Directions:

1. Add mirin and tamari to skillet and bring to a boil over medium-high heat.
2. Add bok choy. Cover and cook until tender when pierced with the tip of a paring knife, 3-5 minutes, discard liquid.

Tips: Mirin is an essential condiment used in Japanese cuisine. It is a kind of rice wine like sake, but with a lower alcohol content and higher sugar content. The sugar is a complex carbohydrate formed naturally via the fermentation process, and therefore, it is not refined sugar. The alcohol content is decreased further when the liquid is heated.

shaved Brussels sprouts

Makes 2 servings

Ingredients:

- 1 teaspoon olive oil
- ¼ cup onion, thinly sliced
- 6 cloves fresh garlic, thinly sliced
- 1-pound Brussels sprouts, thinly sliced (see tip)
- ¼ teaspoon sea salt
- ¼ teaspoon ground black pepper

Directions:

1. Preheat a large cast-iron skillet over medium high heat. The cast iron really works well to get the sprouts nice and crispy.
2. Sauté the onion in the oil for about 3 minutes or until just starting to brown.
3. Add the garlic and sauté for another 30-45 seconds.
4. Add the Brussels sprouts, salt and pepper, and sauté for about 7 minutes or until browned and crisped. Serve.

Tips: To "shave" Brussels sprouts, there is no need to break out a straight edged razor. Trim the nub on the bottom of the sprout and slice the sprout in half. Then just slice the sprouts into thin-as-you-can lengthwise strips. It might take more time, but it's a great way to enjoy these healthy vegetables and well worth the effort. Refrigerate any leftovers.

steamed artichokes

Makes 1 serving

Ingredients:

- 1 artichoke per person

Directions:

1. Slice about ¾ inch off the tip of the artichoke. Pull off any smaller leaves at the base and on the stem. Cut off stem, leaving ½ inch. Rinse artichokes in cold water.
2. Put 2 inches of water into a large pot and insert a steaming basket. Add artichokes and cover. Bring to a boil and reduce heat to simmer. Cook for 25- 35 minutes or until the outer leaves can easily be pulled off.

To eat, pull off outer petals, one at a time. Dip wide fleshy end in melted butter or sauce. Place in mouth, dip side down, and pull through teeth to remove soft, pulpy, delicious portion of the petal. Discard remaining petal. Continue until all the petals are removed.

With a knife or spoon, scrape out ,and discard the inedible fuzzy part (called the "choke") covering the artichoke heart. The remaining bottom of the artichoke is the heart. Cut into pieces and dip into sauce to eat.

Tips: Artichokes may be eaten cold or hot. They are often served either with a healthy plant-based mayonnaise.

baby greens with blackberry vinaigrette

Makes 4 servings

Ingredients:

Dressing:
- ¼ cup fresh or frozen blackberries (defrost if frozen)
- 1 tsp coarsely chopped shallots
- 1 tbsp extra-virgin olive oil
- 2 tbsps fresh lemon juice
- 1 tsp balsamic vinegar
- ¼ tsp Dijon-style mustard
- 1 pinch sea salt
- 1 pinch freshly ground pepper

Salad:
- 4 cups lightly packed mesclun salad mix
- 3 tbsps. chopped walnuts

Directions:

1. Place all dressing ingredients in blender or mini food processor and blend until dressing is creamy and smooth. Let dressing stand in refrigerator for up to 24 hours before using.
2. When ready to serve salad, divide salad greens between 2 plates. Drizzle 2 tbsps. of dressing over each salad. Top with chopped walnuts.

garlic mashed cauliflower

Makes 4 servings

Ingredients:

- 1 medium head cauliflower
- 2 tablespoons virgin organic coconut oil
- 3 tbsps. canned coconut milk
- ¼ tsp sea salt
- 1 clove fresh garlic (or 1 tsp garlic powder)
- ¼ tsp black pepper

Directions:

1. Cut cauliflower into 4-6 pieces and steam until cooked but not overdone.
2. Place in food processor with remaining ingredients, including herbs of your choice, and blend until cauliflower is the consistency of mashed potatoes. Serve immediately.

miso lemon asparagus

Makes 6 servings (1 serving = ¾ cup)

Ingredients:

- 2 bunches asparagus, ends snapped off and cut into 1-2-inch pieces
- ¼ cup water
- 3 garlic cloves, minced
- 2 tbsps. olive oil
- 2 tbsps. lemon juice
- 1 tbsp miso

Directions:

1. Bring water to a boil in a large skillet or wok, over medium high heat. Add asparagus and cook for about 2 mins or until bright green but still a little crunchy. Remove from heat, drain, and set aside.
2. Sauté garlic in olive oil for 2-3 mins in a small sauté pan over medium heat, being careful not to burn the garlic. Remove from heat and add lemon juice and miso, stirring until well mixed. Pour over asparagus and serve immediately.

mushroom and bell pepper sauté with arugula

Makes 4 servings

Ingredients:

- 3 tbsps. olive oil, divided
- ½ pound cremini mushrooms, cut in half, or 2 medium portabellas, thinly
- sliced
- 1 large bell pepper (red, orange, or yellow), sliced very thin
- 2 cloves garlic, minced
- ¼ cup chopped fresh basil leaves (or 1 tbsp dried)
- 1 tbsp balsamic vinegar
- 1tbsp lemon juice
- 4 cups arugula leaves (or any combination of mixed greens)

Directions:

1. Heat 2 tbsps. olive oil over medium heat in a large skillet.
2. Add mushrooms and bell peppers, and sauté until tender, about 7-10 mins.
3. Add garlic, and sauté for 1 more min.
4. Stir in the fresh or dried basil, balsamic vinegar, and lemon juice, cooking over low heat until liquid is reduced by half, about 2 mins.
5. Divide greens among 4 plates, and drizzle with the remaining 1 tbsp olive oil. Top with warm peppers and mushrooms and serve immediately.

roasted balsamic vegetables

Makes 6 servings (1 serving = ¾ cup)

Ingredients:

- 2 lbs. seasonal non-starchy vegetables (broccoli, cauliflower, summer squash,
- mushrooms, etc.)
- ⅓ cup olive oil
- ½ tsp sea salt
- ½ tsp black pepper
- ⅓ cup chopped fresh herbs
- 1 tbsp balsamic vinegar

Directions:

1. Preheat the oven to 425 degrees F.
2. Chop vegetables so that all pieces are approximately the same size. This will ensure all vegetables finish cooking at the same time.
3. Toss together all ingredients except balsamic vinegar and spread in a single layer on a large roasting pan or cookie sheet.
4. Stirring occasionally, roast the vegetables for 30-35 mins or until cooked through and browned.
5. Just prior to serving, drizzle with balsamic vinegar.

sesame broccoli

Makes 4 servings

Ingredients:

- 2 heads of broccoli
- ½ cup water
- ¼ tsp sea salt
- 2 tbsps. olive oil
- 3 cloves garlic, slivered
- 3 green onions sliced thin
- 2 tbsp lemon juice
- ¾ tsp turmeric
- 1 tbsp sesame seeds
- 1 tbsp sesame oil

Directions:

1. Cut broccoli into bite-sized florets. Cut the stems into small pieces and peel if they are tough. You should have a total of 6-8 cups.
2. In a large skillet, bring ½ cup water to boil. Add broccoli and sprinkle with salt. Cover and cook about 4 mins, until broccoli is slightly tender but not soft. The water will have evaporated. Remove from pan to a serving dish.
3. Add olive oil to the skillet and sauté garlic and green onions over low heat for 3 mins. Return broccoli to skillet. Add lemon juice and turmeric. Cook for 2 more mins until broccoli is warmed.
4. Sprinkle with sesame seeds. Return to serving dish and drizzle sesame oil over broccoli before serving.

baked jicama fries

Makes 4 servings

Ingredients:

- 1 medium jicama
- ½ tsp turmeric
- ¼ tsp sea salt
- ¼ tsp black pepper
- 1 ½ tsp unrefined organic coconut oil, melted

Directions:

1. Preheat oven to 400 degrees F and line baking sheet with parchment paper.
2. Scrub, rinse, and peel the jicama. Slice into French fry-sized pieces and gently pat dry (they can remain slightly damp). Place on the lined baking sheet.
3. In a small bowl, mix the turmeric, sea salt, and black pepper. Set aside.
4. Drizzle the melted coconut oil over the jicama. Gently toss to coat. Sprinkle the spice mixture over the jicama and gently toss again until the jicama is evenly coated. Spread out the jicama in a single layer on the baking sheet.
5. Bake for 40 mins (or until it reaches the desired texture). Halfway through cooking time, flip jicama fries to brown evenly.

baked zesty carrot fries

Makes 4 servings

Ingredients:

- 5 large carrots
- 1 tsp extra-virgin olive oil
- ¼ tsp chili powder*
- 1 pinch cinnamon
- ⅛ tsp sea salt

Directions:

1. Preheat oven to 400 degrees F.
2. Peel carrots and slice into chips or French fry-sized pieces. Place carrots on a cookie sheet and drizzle with the olive oil. Sprinkle chili powder and cinnamon evenly over the carrots, then toss to coat.
3. Bake for 20-25 mins or until carrots are at desired tenderness.

Tips:
A mandolin-type vegetable slicer works well for slicing carrots.
*Omit chili powder if avoiding nightshades.

cauliflower rice

Makes 4 servings

Ingredients:

- 1 head cauliflower
- 2 tbsps. extra-virgin olive oil or unrefined, organic coconut oil
- 1 small yellow onion, finely chopped
- 1 pinch sea salt

Optional Ingredients:
- 1 tbsp lime juice (juice of ½ lime)
- 1 pinch cumin
- 1 tbsps. chopped fresh cilantro

Directions:

1. Cut the cauliflower in half. Place a box grater over a large bowl and grate each cauliflower half using the biggest holes of the grater, holding the cauliflower by its stem as you grate. Alternatively, you can coarsely chop the core and the florets and pulse them together in a food processor until they are reduced to the size of couscous or rice grains. Be careful not to over-process.
2. Heat the oil in a medium nonstick pan over medium-high heat until shimmering. Add the onion and cook until softened, 2 to 3 mins.
3. Put the cauliflower "rice" in the pan and stir to combine. Cook, stirring frequently, until the cauliflower is slightly crispy on the outside but tender on the inside, 5 to 8 mins.
4. To enhance the flavor, add the salt, lime juice, cumin, and/or cilantro and serve.

roasted beets & greens

Makes 4 servings

Ingredients:

- 1-2 bunches trimmed beets (about 4-8 medium beets)
- 1 ½ tbsps. extra-virgin olive oil
- 1 lemon, juiced (approx. 3 tbsps. juice)
- 2 tsps. coconut aminos
- 1 clove garlic, minced
- ¼ tsp sea salt
- ¼ tsp black pepper
- 4 cups baby spinach or spring mix, divided
- 1 cup fresh parsley
- ¼ large red onion, sliced

Directions:

1. Preheat oven to 400 degrees F.
2. Rinse and dry beets, then wrap each one in foil.
3. Roast until tender (about 1 hour). Let cool, then peel and dice.
4. Whisk together olive oil, lemon juice, coconut aminos, garlic, sea salt, and pepper. Toss with beets.
5. For each serving, toss ½ cup dressed beets with 1 cup spinach or spring mix and 14 cup parsley. Top with red onion slices.

roasted radishes

Makes 4 servings

Ingredients:

- 4 cups radishes (about 3 bunches), trimmed and quartered
- 2 tbsps. unrefined coconut oil, melted
- ½ tsp salt

Directions:

1. Preheat the oven to 375 degrees F. Line a rimmed baking sheet with parchment paper or silicone liner for easier cleanup.
2. In a small bowl, toss the radishes with the coconut oil.
3. Spread in a single layer on the prepared baking sheet and sprinkle with the salt.
4. Roast for 20 to 25 mins, until the radishes are fork-tender and start to turn golden brown.

Tips: Roasted radishes have a texture that is like potatoes. Daikon radishes can be used in place of regular radishes to enhance nutritional density and support detoxification pathways.

sautéed Swiss chard

Makes 4 servings

Ingredients:

- 1 lb. Swiss chard (about 1 large bunch), well rinsed
- 1 tbsp extra-virgin olive oil
- 1 tbsp unrefined coconut oil
- 1 medium onion, sliced thin in rings cut in half
- 1 clove garlic, finely chopped
- ¼ tsp black pepper

Directions:

1. Cut stems and center ribs from chard, discarding any tough portions, then cut stems and ribs crosswise into 2-inch pieces. Stack chard leaves and roll up lengthwise into tight cylinders. Cut cylinders crosswise to make 1-inch-wide strips.
2. Heat olive oil and coconut oil in a large heavy pot over medium heat until foam subsides, then cook onions and garlic, occasionally stirring, until onions begin to soften, about 8 mins.
3. Add chard stems, ribs, and pepper to the pot. Cover and cook, occasionally stirring, until stems are just tender, about 10 mins.
4. Add chard leaves in batches, stirring each until wilted before adding next batch. Cover and cook occasionally stirring until tender, 4 to 6 mins. Transfer with the sauteed stems and ribs to a bowl and serve.

Tips: Chard can be washed, dried, and cut two days ahead and chilled in sealed bags lined with dampened paper towels. Chard can be cooked four hours ahead and reheated over low heat on stove or in a microwave oven.

shaved Brussels sprouts with leeks & pomegranate

Makes 6 servings (1 serving = ¾ to 1 cup)

Ingredients:

- 2 lbs. Brussels sprouts
- 1 tbsp extra-virgin olive oil
- 1 leek, sliced, white part only
- 2 cloves garlic, minced
- ⅔ cup vegetable broth
- ¾ tsp sea salt
- ½ tsp black pepper
- ¼ cup pomegranate seeds

shaved Brussels sprouts with leeks & pomegranate

Directions:

1. Shred the Brussels sprouts using the greater attachment on a food processor or a mandolin.
2. Put olive oil in a large saucepan or stockpot over medium-high heat.
3. Place the Brussels sprouts, leek, and garlic in the saucepan. Sauté for 5 mins.
4. Add the broth, salt, and pepper. Cover and steam for 5 mins, until the Brussels sprouts are bright green and tender, and most of the broth is cooked down.
5. Garnish with pomegranate seeds and serve warm.

steamed spinach with fresh lemon

Makes 2 servings

Ingredients:

- 9 oz baby or trimmed regular spinach
- 1 tbsp fresh lemon juice, plus lemon wedges for garnish
- ⅛ tsp sea salt

Directions:

1. Fill a medium saucepan with about 1-2 inches of water and fit with a steamer insert. Bring to a boil, add spinach, and reduce to a simmer. Cover and steam until spinach has wilted, about 2 mins.
2. Transfer spinach to a glass serving bowl. Toss with oil, lemon juice, and salt. Garnish with lemon wedges. Serve immediately.

arugula and baby greens

Makes 4 servings

Ingredients:

- 4 cups arugula
- 4 cups baby greens
- 3 teaspoons lemon juice
- ⅛ teaspoon garlic powder or ½ clove fresh garlic
- ½ teaspoon finely grated lemon zest (optional)
- 4 teaspoons extra-virgin olive oil
- Salt & pepper to taste

Directions:

1. Combine arugula and baby greens in a large bowl.
2. In a separate bowl, whisk together lemon juice, garlic, lemon zest, extra-virgin olive oil, salt, and pepper.
3. Toss salad with vinaigrette and divide into four portions.
4. Serve immediately.

lime-scented coconut rice

Makes 6 servings (1 serving ≈ ½ cup)

Ingredients:

- 2 tablespoons extra-virgin olive oil
- 2 tablespoons minced onion
- 1 teaspoon minced garlic
- 1 cup brown basmati rice
- ¾ cup vegetable broth
- ¾ cup canned lite coconut milk
- ½ cup water
- ½ teaspoon sea salt
- ¼ cup finely chopped raw, unsalted cashews
- ½ cup thinly sliced scallions
- ¼ cup minced cilantro
- 1 tablespoon fresh lime juice

Directions:

1. In a medium saucepan, heat oil over medium heat.
2. Add onion and sauté for about 3 minutes, or until translucent.
3. Add garlic and cook for 30 seconds more.
4. Add the rice, stirring to coat with oil. Add broth, coconut milk, water, and sea salt. Bring to a simmer. Cover and cook for 40–60 minutes, or until liquid is absorbed. Remove from heat.
5. While rice is cooking, toast the cashews. Using a small skillet, toast nuts over medium-low heat for about 5 minutes, or until lightly browned. Stir frequently and watch closely to prevent burning. When toasted, remove to a plate to cool.
6. When the rice is done, fluff with a fork. Stir in scallions, cilantro, and lime juice.
7. Serve garnished with toasted cashews.

Soups

Soups

oven-baked lentil and split pea soup

Makes 8 servings (1 serving ≈ 1 ½ cups)

Ingredients:

- 1 cup split peas, rinsed well
- 1 cup lentils, rinsed well
- 10 cups vegetable broth
- 2 medium carrots, sliced or diced
- 2 celery stalks, sliced or diced
- 1 large red bell pepper, chopped (1 ½ -2 cups)
- 1 large onion, chopped
- 1 bay leaf
- 1 teaspoon cumin
- ¼ teaspoon ground black pepper
- ½ teaspoon salt

Directions:

1. Put peas and lentils in a Dutch oven or large oven-proof pot.
2. Add remaining ingredients and bake, covered, in 350 degrees F oven for about 2 hours or until lentils and peas are tender.
3. Alternatively, you can cook for 1 hour on top of the stove, stirring occasionally. Remove bay leaf before serving.

sweet potato and kale soup

Makes 4 servings

Ingredients:

- 1 medium onion, coarsely chopped
- 1 clove minced garlic
- 1 red or yellow bell pepper, chopped
- 3 medium sweet potatoes or yams, peeled and cubed
- 5 cups vegetable broth
- ¼ teaspoon sea salt
- ¼ teaspoon freshly ground black pepper
- 1 can coconut milk
- 1 bunch dinosaur kale, de-stemmed and thinly sliced (about 5-6 cups)
- Optional garnish: parsley and red pepper flakes

Directions:

1. In a heavy soup pot, add onion, garlic, bell peppers, sweet potatoes, and broth. Bring to a boil. Reduce heat and simmer for 5 minutes.
2. Add coconut milk and kale and cook about 3-4 minutes.
3. Soup is ready when all vegetables are soft.
4. Garnish with parsley and red pepper flakes.

Tips:
Serve soup over brown rice or quinoa.
Or serve over cauliflower rice for a lower-carb meal.

black soybean cocoa soup with lime zest

Makes 4 servings

Ingredients:

- 1 tablespoon extra-virgin olive oil
- 1 small red onion, chopped
- 3 cloves garlic, pressed
- 1 large carrot, chopped
- 1 stalk celery, chopped
- 3 cups vegetable broth
- 2 tablespoons unsweetened cocoa powder
- 1 teaspoon cumin
- 1 cup canned black beans, drained and rinsed
- 1 cup canned black soybeans, drained and rinsed
- Grated zest of 1 lime
- 2-4 tablespoons fresh cilantro, chopped

Directions:

1. In a medium saucepan, heat olive oil over low heat. Add the onion and sauté until the onions are caramelized, for approximately 15 minutes.
2. Add the pressed garlic, carrots, and celery, and cook for 5 minutes longer.
3. Add the broth, cocoa powder, and cumin. Stir well, and simmer for 10 more minutes.
4. Stir in the black beans and black soybeans. Add lime zest. Cook for approximately 20 minutes or longer, over low heat.
5. Serve warm, garnished with chopped cilantro.

Tips: This recipe is wonderful topped with sliced avocado or fresh guacamole

ten vegetable soup with tempeh

Makes 8 servings (1 serving ≈ 1 ½ cups)

Ingredients:

- 2 tablespoons extra virgin olive oil
- 3 cups chopped green cabbage, quartered
- 1 cup cauliflower florets, 1-inch pieces
- 1 medium leek, sliced (use white and 1 inch of light green part)
- 1 small onion, chopped
- 1 medium carrot, chopped
- 1 medium celery stalk, chopped
- 1 can (14.5 ounces) diced tomatoes (no salt added)
- 4 cups vegetable broth
- 1 medium yellow-fleshed potato, diced
- ¼ cup chopped flat-leaf parsley (fresh)
- 1 tablespoon dried thyme
- 1 ½ cups packed Swiss chard or spinach, cut crosswise into ½ -inch strips
- 2 cups tempeh
- ½ teaspoon sea salt
- ¼ teaspoon freshly ground pepper
- Pinch red pepper flakes or cayenne

ten vegetable soup with tempeh

Directions:

1. Using a large Dutch oven or heavy soup pot with tight-fitting cover, heat oil over medium heat.
2. Add cabbage, cauliflower, leek, onion, carrot, and celery. Stirring occasionally, cook vegetables until about 8 minutes (until vegetables release their juices).
3. Add tomatoes (with the liquid), broth, potato, parsley, and thyme. Increase heat to medium-high until liquid boils. Cover, reduce heat, and simmer soup for 10 minutes.
4. Add Swiss chard and tempeh, and simmer for 10 minutes. Season soup with sea salt and pepper (and red pepper flakes, if desired). Let sit for 15 minutes before serving.

Tips: If desired, refrigerate for up to 4 days, reheating in covered pot over medium heat. Or divide cooled soup among re-sealable freezer bags and freeze. This soup keeps in freezer for up to 2 months.

beans and greens soup

Makes 8 servings (1 serving ≈ 1 ½ cups)

Ingredients:

- 4 cups sliced yellow onions (approximately 3 onions)
- ¼ cup extra virgin olive oil
- 3 garlic cloves, minced
- 2 (15 ounces) cans white cannellini beans, drained & rinsed
- 1 large branch fresh rosemary (6-7 inches)
- 2 quarts vegetable broth
- 1 bay leaf
- 6 cups chopped greens such as escarole, spinach, bok choy or kale
- ½ teaspoon sea salt
- ½ teaspoon black pepper

Directions:

1. In a large stockpot over low to medium heat, sauté the onions with the olive oil until the onions are translucent, about 5-10 minutes.
2. Add the garlic and cook over low heat for 2 more minutes.
3. Add the drained white beans, rosemary, broth, and bay leaf. Cover bring to a boil, and simmer for 30-40 minutes, until the beans are very soft.
4. Remove the rosemary branch and the bay leaf. In small batches, puree in a food processor, or leave soup in pot and use hand blender to puree.
5. Return soup to the pot to reheat. Add greens and cook until they are wilted. If you are using escarole or kale, they will need a few minutes longer than more tender greens. Season with salt and pepper.

black soybean and quinoa soup

Makes 8 servings (1 serving ≈ 1 ½ -2 cups)

Ingredients:

- 1 large onion, chopped
- 2 tablespoons olive oil
- 4 cloves garlic, minced
- 2 poblano pepper, seeded & chopped
- 2 jalapeno pepper, seeded & chopped
- 6 cups water or vegetable broth
- 3 cans (16 ounces) black soybeans, drained
- 2 teaspoons ground cumin
- 1 bunch cilantro, including stems
- 1 teaspoon sea salt
- 2 cups cooked quinoa or brown rice

Directions:

1. Sauté onion in olive oil until soft. Add garlic and sauté briefly. Add poblano and jalapeno peppers and continue to sauté for about 5 more minutes.
2. Add remaining ingredients, except for quinoa or rice, and simmer, covered for 20 minutes. Add cooked quinoa or rice and simmer for another 5 minutes. Adjust seasonings and cool
3. In small batches, puree ½ of the soup in the food processor and return to the soup pot. Mix well and reheat before serving.

miso soup

Makes 4 servings

Ingredients:

- 6 cups water
- 2 medium carrots, grated or finely chopped
- 12 oz silken tofu (extra firm)
- 3-inch strip of wakame seaweed, cut into small pieces with kitchen scissors
- 1 tbsp low-sodium, gluten-free tamari
- 1 large handful of baby spinach leaves
- ¼ cup miso, any flavor variety
- ⅓ cup hot water
- 3 scallions, thinly sliced on the diagonal

Directions:

1. Bring 6 cups water to a boil in a soup pot. Add carrots, tofu, wakame, and tamari. Lower heat to a simmer and cook for about 10 mins. Remove from heat and add spinach; set aside. Spinach will wilt on its own.
2. Dissolve miso in ⅓ cup hot water. When serving soup, add 1 heaping tbsp of miso mixture to each bowl, and garnish with sliced scallions. Serve immediately.

Tips: If there are any leftovers, refrigerate soup and dissolved miso separately, combining them after heating soup so as not to destroy the live organisms in the miso.

curried broccoli soup

Makes 6 servings (1 serving = approximately 1 cup or 8 oz)

Ingredients:

- 2 tbsps organic coconut oil
- 4 leeks, white and light-green ends only, cleaned, trimmed, and thinly sliced
- 1 large yellow onion, roughly chopped
- 3 medium shallots, roughly chopped
- 1 ½ lbs. broccoli, trimmed and cut into uniform-sized pieces
- 4 cups vegetable broth
- 12 oz silken tofu (extra firm)
- 1 tbsp curry powder*
- ½ tsp sea salt
- ¼ tsp black pepper
- 1 cup full-fat coconut milk

Directions:

1. In a large stockpot, melt the coconut oil over medium heat.
2. Add the leeks, onion, and shallots, and sauté until softened, 5 to 10 mins. Toss in the chopped broccoli, tofu, and add the broth. Top off with some water if the vegetables aren't fully submerged. Bring the soup to a boil over high heat, and then lower the heat to a simmer. Continue cooking for 20 mins or until the vegetables are soft.
3. Add the curry powder and season with salt and pepper to taste. Turn off the burner and cool the soup slightly. Use an immersion blender to puree the ingredients together or put divided portions into a blender and puree until smooth.
4. Return soup to pan, add the coconut milk, and stir to incorporate. Turn the heat up to a medium high to bring the soup back to a boil before serving.

*Use nightshade-free curry powder if avoiding nightshades

Main Dishes

Main Dishes

nutty green rice

Makes 8 servings (1 serving ≈ ½ cup)

Ingredients:

- 1 cup basmati or brown rice
- 2 cup water
- ¼ teaspoon salt
- ½ cup almonds
- 1 bunch parsley
- 1 clove garlic
- 1 ½ tablespoons lemon juice
- 1 ½ tablespoons olive oil
- ¼ teaspoon freshly ground pepper
- ½ cucumber, diced, for garnish

Directions:

1. Bring water to a boil, add rice and salt, stir and simmer, covered for 45 minutes. Do not stir again. Remove from heat and let sit for another 10 minutes; then remove cover and allow to cool.
2. While rice is cooking, blend almonds, parsley, garlic, lemon juice, olive oil and pepper in a food processor.
3. When rice is cool, stir with nut mixture.
4. Garnish with cucumber, if desired.

quick brown rice and black bean bowl

Makes 4 servings

Ingredients:

- 4 teaspoons coconut oil
- 2 cups chopped baby spinach
- 2 cups cooked brown rice
- 2 cups canned black beans, rinsed, and drained
- 1 teaspoon sea salt
- 1 teaspoon garlic powder
- 1 teaspoon cumin
- 1 avocado, chopped
- 1 cup chopped tomatoes

Directions:

1. Heat a large pan on medium-high heat. Add coconut oil to the pan, and melt. Add spinach and sauté until wilted.
2. Add rice, beans, sea salt, garlic powder, and cumin. Cook until all ingredients are heated through. Remove from heat.
3. Right before serving, gently fold in avocado and tomatoes.

cilantro lime cauliflower rice

Makes 6 servings (1 serving ≈ ½ cup)

Ingredients:

- 1 head cauliflower (≈ 24 ounces or 6 cups chopped)
- 1 tablespoon extra-virgin olive oil
- 2 cloves garlic
- 2 scallions, diced
- ¼ teaspoon sea salt
- ¼ teaspoon pepper
- 3 tablespoons fresh lime juice (juice of 1 ½ limes)
- ¼ cups fresh chopped cilantro

Directions:

1. Rinse cauliflower, and pat dry. Chop into florets, and grate in food processor. If you don't have a food processor, leave cauliflower whole, and grate with box grater. The cauliflower should resemble the size of rice or couscous.
2. Heat a large pan on medium heat, and add olive oil, garlic, and scallions. Sauté 3-4 minutes.
3. Increase heat to medium-high and add cauliflower. Sauté for 5-6 minutes; remove from heat and transfer to a large bowl (before cauliflower gets mushy).
4. Toss with sea salt, pepper, lime juice, and cilantro.

three bean vegetable chili

Makes 6 servings (1 serving ≈ 1 ¾ cups)

Ingredients:

- 1 tablespoon olive oil
- ½ large onion, diced
- 2 carrots, diced
- 1 red bell pepper, chopped
- 1 clove garlic, finely chopped
- 1 jalapeno pepper, seeded and minced
- 1 ½ tablespoons chili powder
- 2 teaspoons ground cumin
- 1 ½ teaspoons dried oregano
- 1 can (28 ounces) no-salt added diced tomatoes
- 1 cup water
- 1 can (15 ounces) black beans, rinsed and drained
- 1 can (15 ounces) red kidney beans, rinsed and drained
- 1 can (15 ounces) Great Northern beans, rinsed and drained
- ½ teaspoon sea salt

Garnish:

- Fresh cilantro
- Chopped scallions

Directions:

1. Heat oil in large saucepan or stockpot. Add onions, carrots, bell peppers, garlic, and jalapeno and cook until onion is translucent (about 5 minutes).
2. Add dry spices (chili powder, cumin, and oregano), and cook for a 1 minute, stirring frequently.
3. Add canned tomatoes including juices, water, beans, and salt. Bring to boil, reduce heat, and then simmer uncovered for 30 minutes.
4. Serve garnished with chopped cilantro and scallions.

Tips: Try to find low-sodium canned beans. Otherwise, be sure to rinse beans well after draining to reduce sodium.

greek lentil stew

Makes 4 servings

Ingredients:

- 1 tablespoon extra-virgin olive oil
- 1 small red onion, chopped
- 1 medium yellow sweet pepper, chopped
- 2 cloves garlic, finely chopped
- 1 cup lentils
- 2 teaspoons dried oregano
- 1 teaspoons ground cinnamon
- 2 ½ cups low-sodium vegetable broth, divided
- 1 medium zucchini squash, chopped
- 1 medium yellow squash, chopped
- 1 tablespoon tomato paste
- ½ cup unsweetened pomegranate juice
- ½ teaspoon sea salt
- ¼ teaspoon black pepper

Directions:

1. In a small Dutch oven, heat oil over medium-high heat. Add onion and bell pepper, and sauté for 1 minute. Cover pot tightly and cook over medium heat for 4 minutes. Add garlic and cook for 1 minute longer.
2. Stir in lentils, oregano, and cinnamon, and cook until seasoning is fragrant.
3. Add 2 cups of broth. Bring to a boil, reduce heat, and cover. Simmer lentils for 25 minutes.
4. Add zucchini and yellow squash, tomato paste, pomegranate juice, remaining broth, sea salt, and pepper. Simmer for 15 minutes, or until lentils are done to your taste.
5. Let stew sit, uncovered, for 15 minutes. Serve warm or at room temperature, divided among soup bowls.

Thai barley and veggie stir-fry with edamame

Makes 4 servings

Ingredients:

- ½ cup pearled barley
- 1 cup water
- 1 tablespoon coconut oil, divided
- 2 cloves garlic, finely chopped
- 1 cup thinly sliced Chinese or regular eggplant
- ½ cup chopped red bell pepper
- ½ cup chopped onion
- 1 cup green soybeans (edamame)
- 3 tablespoons chopped fresh basil leaves
- 1 tablespoon chopped fresh mint leaves
- 8 to 10 drops red pepper hot sauce
- 1 teaspoon low sodium soy sauce
- 2 tablespoon chopped unsalted cashews
- ½ cup shredded red cabbage
- ½ cup shredded carrots

Directions:

1. In a medium saucepan, combine barley and water, and bring to a boil. Reduce heat to low, cover, and then cook for 45 minutes or until the barley is tender and liquid is absorbed. Set aside.
2. In a large skillet or wok, heat 1 tablespoon of the coconut oil over medium-high heat. Add garlic and stir-fry for 3 to 4 minutes. Add the cooked barley and stir-fry an additional 3 minutes. Transfer mixture to a dish and set aside.
3. Return the same skillet to stove and heat the remaining tablespoon of coconut oil over high heat. Add the eggplant, bell pepper, onion, and soybeans, and stir-fry 3 to 4 minutes.
4. Add basil, mint, hot sauce, and soy sauce. Cook for about 2 minutes.
5. Add the barley and garlic mixture back to the pan, and heat for 3 minutes, stirring frequently.
6. Garnish by topping with chopped cashews, shredded red cabbage, and shredded carrots.

curried vegetable stew

Makes 6 servings (1 serving ≈ 1 ¼ cups)

Ingredients:

- 2 medium-large onions, diced
- 1 ½ tablespoons, coconut, or olive oil
- 3 garlic cloves, minced
- 6 small new potatoes, unpeeled, washed and diced
- 4 medium carrots, scrubbed & sliced
- 2 cups water
- 1 small head cauliflower or broccoli, cut into bite-sized pieces
- 1 bunch baby bok choy, chopped
- 2 cups fresh green beans, cut into 1-inch pieces (or one 10 ounces package frozen cut green beans, thawed)
- 2-3 teaspoons grated fresh ginger
- 1-2 teaspoons curry powder
- 3 teaspoons ground turmeric
- 1 can (15-ounces) lite coconut milk
- 1-2 tablespoons red curry paste, for those who prefer a zippier taste
- 1 ½ cups frozen baby peas, thawed
- ½ teaspoon sea salt

Directions:

1. Sauté onion in oil for 3-4 minutes over medium heat in a large, heavy soup pot.
2. Add garlic and sauté another minute.
3. Now add potatoes, carrots, and 2 cups water. Bring to a simmer and cover. Cook for about 10 minutes. Potatoes will not be fully cooked yet.
4. Add the cauliflower, bok choy, green beans, ginger, and spices. Cover and continue simmering gently for about 10-15 minutes, until veggies are tender. Mash some of the potatoes against the side of the pot to thicken the soup.
5. Now stir in the coconut milk and the curry paste, if using, being sure that the paste is well mixed in.
6. Allow to simmer (on low heat) for 5-10 minutes and then turn off heat and let sit to blend flavors until ready to serve. Just before serving, stir in defrosted frozen baby peas (at about room temperature), adding some sea salt to taste if needed.

mushroom and pepper sauté with arugula

Makes 6 servings (1 serving ≈ ¾ cup)

Ingredients:

- 3 tablespoons olive oil, divided
- ½ pound cremini mushrooms, cut in half or 2 medium portabellas, thinly sliced
- 1 large or 2 small yellow, red, or orange bell peppers, sliced very thin
- 2 cloves garlic, minced
- 1 tablespoon balsamic vinegar
- 1 tablespoon lemon juice
- ¼ cup fresh basil leaves, chopped (or 1 tablespoon dried)
- 1 pinch sea salt
- 4 cups arugula leaves (or any combinations of mixed greens

Directions:

1. Heat 2 tablespoons olive oil over medium heat in a large skillet.
2. Add mushrooms, and bell peppers, and sauté until tender, about 7-10 minutes.
3. Add garlic and sauté for one more minute.
4. Stir in the fresh or dried basil (if using), along with a pinch of salt if needed.
5. Divide greens among four plates and drizzle with the remaining one tablespoon of olive oil. Top with warm peppers and mushrooms and serve immediately.

kasha, potatoes, and mushrooms

Makes 6 servings (1 serving ≈ ¾ cup)

Ingredients:

- 1 tablespoon extra-virgin olive oil
- 1 small onion, chopped fine
- 2 cloves garlic, minced
- 1 teaspoon sea salt
- 1 small red potato or yam, ¼-inch dice
- 6 crimini mushrooms, chopped fine
- 1 cup kasha
- 2 cups boiling water
- ¼ teaspoon freshly ground pepper

Directions:

1. In a 3-4-quart heavy pot with a tight-fitting lid, heat the oil over medium heat. Add onions, garlic, and salt, and sauté until the onion is golden and soft. This will take at least 10 minutes. The more caramelized the onions, the better the flavor.
2. Add 2 cups of water to a tea kettle and bring to a boil.
3. While the water is heating, add finely chopped potatoes and mushrooms. Sauté for 3-4 minutes, covered, until juicy. Add kasha to the mixture and stir, coating the kasha.
4. Pour in boiling water and turn the heat to low. Cover pot, and simmer for about 15 minutes on low until water is absorbed. Remove the lid and allow kasha to rest for 10 more minutes. Add pepper and stir.

bruschetta spaghetti squash

Makes 6 servings (1 serving = 1 cup)

Ingredients:

- 1 medium spaghetti squash
- 2 tbsps olive oil
- 2 cups cherry tomatoes
- ¼ cup red onion, finely diced
- 2 garlic cloves, minced
- 2 tbsps fresh basil, cut julienne-style
- 2 tbsps. balsamic vinegar
- ½ tsp sea salt
- ¼ tsp cracked black pepper
- ¼ cup extra-virgin olive oil

Directions:

1. Preheat oven to 350 degrees F. Prepare the squash by rinsing, drying, and poking it 3-4 times with a fork or knife. Bake for 45-55 mins. It is done when a knife can be inserted easily (be careful not to overcook till too soft on the inside). Remove from oven, set aside, and allow to cool completely.
2. Cut the squash in half lengthwise. Remove the seeds by hand or with a spoon. Then take a fork and scrape the inside of the squash, filling a bowl with the "shreds." Drizzle 2 tbsps. olive oil over the shredded squash and toss. Set aside.
3. Cut the tomatoes into quarters and set aside. In a medium bowl, mix garlic, basil, balsamic vinegar, sea salt, and black pepper. Whisk in ¼ cup olive oil (slowly streaming in the oil while whisking). Add the cut omatoes to the dressing. Allow to marinate for 15-20 mins.
4. Toss the tomato mixture with spaghetti squash. Serve cold or warm (gently reheated).

Tips: This can be made in advance, but do not toss the squash and tomato mixture together until ready to serve.

edamame collard wrap

Makes 6 servings (1 serving = 1 wrap)

Ingredients:

- 10-oz bag frozen, shelled organic, edamame (= 2 ¼ cups)
- 4 cups water, divided
- ¾ tsp plus 1 pinch sea salt, divided
- 6 collard leaves
- ¼ cup tahini
- ¼ cup fresh lemon juice
- 2 cloves garlic
- 2 tbsps. extra-virgin olive oil
- 12 red pepper strips
- 1 tomato, sliced thin, and each slice halved
- 1 avocado, sliced into 6 portions

Directions:

1. In a medium saucepan, cook edamame in 2 cups boiling water for about 5 mins. Drain and set aside to cool.
2. In a large sauté pan or medium stockpot, bring 2 cups water to a boil. Add a pinch of sea salt. Place the collard greens in the water, cover, and turn off heat. Allow to sit for 1 min. Rinse the collard leaves under cold water, drain, lightly pat dry, and set aside.
3. Put the cooled edamame in a food processor with the tahini, remaining ¾ tsp sea salt, lemon juice, and garlic. Blend for about 10 secs. Add olive oil slowly thru the tube while the processor is running. Add more olive oil if consistency is not smooth and creamy. Adjust seasonings, if needed.
4. On a large cutting board, or on individual plates, lay out each steamed collard leaf. Evenly divide the red peppers, avocado, and hummus among the 6 collard leaves. Roll the collard leaves as you would a tortilla and enjoy.

Tips: The edamame filling can be enjoyed as a hummus with brain-friendly cruciferous veggies for dipping, such as daikon radish, kohlrabi, and cauliflower.

vegetable shirataki noodle stir-fry

Makes 4 servings

Ingredients::

- 3 tbsps toasted sesame oil, divided
- 1 medium onion, thinly sliced and halved
- 2-3 garlic cloves, minced
- ¼ lb fresh shiitake mushrooms, stems discarded, caps sliced
- 2-3 tbsps coconut aminos
- ½ lb fresh or frozen broccoli, cut into small florets
- 4 oz bamboo shoots, sliced
- 1 tbsp fresh ginger, grated
- 2 tsps sesame seeds
- ½ tsp red pepper flakes*
- 1-quart water
- 16 oz shirataki noodles

Directions:

1. In a large skillet or wok, heat 2 tbsps of the sesame oil over medium heat. Add the onions, garlic, shiitake mushrooms, and coconut aminos. Cook until onions are tender. (If the pan becomes too dry, add some water.)
2. Add the remaining sesame oil to the skillet, then add the broccoli, bamboo shoots, ginger, sesame seeds, and pepper flakes. Stir until the broccoli is crisp-tender, about 4 to 5 mins.
3. While the vegetables are cooking, bring the water to a boil in a large saucepan. Rinse the shirataki noodles in a colander under running water for about 15 seconds and drain. Add the noodles to the boiling water and cook for 3 mins. Drain the noodles and put back in the dry saucepan over low heat, stirring until the noodles are dry.
4. Add noodles to the vegetables. Toss over medium-high heat until well-blended and heated through.

Tips: Shirataki noodles are a soluble source of plant fiber that helps with appetite control and blood sugar stability.

*Omit red pepper flakes if avoiding nightshades.

zucchini noodles with pesto and organic tempeh

Makes 4 servings

Ingredients:

- 2 cups zucchini, spiral cut or julienned into noodles
- ½ tsp sea salt
- 2 tsp unrefined coconut oil
- 1 medium to large sweet onion, diced
- 8 oz organic tempeh, diced
- 2 tbsps dairy-free pesto

Directions:

1. Place the zucchini in a strainer over a larger bowl or in the sink. Sprinkle with sea salt and toss to coat. Allow the zucchini to sit for 15-20 mins to allow excess liquid to drain.
2. Wrap zucchini in a few paper towels and squeeze gently to remove any remaining moisture. Wrap again in fresh paper towels and set aside.
3. In a large skillet, put the coconut oil. Add onion and sauté over medium heat until translucent. Add tempeh and sauté for 3-5 more mins.
4. Add the zucchini noodles to the skillet and cook for 3-4 mins., occasionally stirring, until the zucchini noodles are tender.
5. Add pesto to the skillet. Toss to coat noodles and serve immediately.

Tips: If you don't own a spiralizer, you can find zucchini already prepared as "zoodles" in some grocery stores. Alternatively, zucchini can be sliced or julienne cut.

zucchini mushroom pasta

Makes 2 servings

Ingredients:

- 1 lb. zucchini
- 3-4 tbsps. extra-virgin olive oil
- 8-10 baby bella or crimini mushrooms, sliced
- 2-3 garlic cloves, minced
- 2 tbsps. chopped fresh basil
- ¼ tsp sea salt
- ¼ tsp black pepper
- ¼ cup store-bought basil pesto (dairy free)

Directions:

1. Peel zucchini using vegetable peeler. Cut lengthwise into ribbons using the vegetable peeler until you reach the seed core.
2. In a large skillet over medium heat, heat 2 tbsps. of the oil. Add the mushrooms and garlic and cook for 2-3 mins.
3. Add the zucchini strands to the skillet and cook until the zucchini softens (5 mins or less). Add the basil, sea salt, and pepper.
4. Gently toss zucchini mixture with pesto.

Tips: Consider purchasing a spiral cutter for processing the zucchini into long shreds that mimic spaghetti. Reserve the zucchini's seed core for another use, such as chopped and added to a salad.

ginger basil vegetable stir fry with mung bean & edamame pasta

Makes 4 servings

Ingredients:

- 8 cup water
- 7.05-oz (200 gram) package of mung bean and edamame pasta
- 4 tbsps. fresh lime juice, plus the zest of half a lime
- 1 tbsp toasted sesame oil
- 2 tbsps. apple cider vinegar
- 3 tbsps. coconut aminos
- 1 tbsp unrefined, organic coconut oil
- 2 cup carrots, cut into matchsticks
- 1 cup (8 ounces) petite green beans, fresh or frozen
- 2 cup baby bok choy, chopped
- 2 tbsps. peeled and chopped fresh ginger
- 3 cloves garlic, minced
- 6 scallions, both dark and light green parts, cut into 1-inch pieces
- ½ cup packed fresh basil, chopped
- ¼ cup chopped raw cashews

Directions:

1.Fill a large saucepan with water and bring to a boil. Add the pasta and return to a boil. Cover the pan and reduce heat to simmer for 7-8 mins or until pasta is al dente. Drain pasta in a fine mesh colander and rinse with cold water. Set aside.

2. Meanwhile, in a small bowl, whisk together lime juice and zest, sesame oil, vinegar, and coconut aminos. Set aside.

3. Melt 1 tbsp coconut oil in a large skillet over medium-high heat. Add carrots, green beans, baby bok choy, ginger, garlic, and scallions. Sauté until vegetables are tender, about 2-4 mins. Add the lime juice mixture to the vegetables and sauté for about 30 more seconds.

4. Add the cooked pasta and toss with tongs until combined. Add chopped basil and cashews and toss again until well combined and heated through (about 1 min).

Tips: Consider using kelp powder to add more flavor and enhance iodine content, if desired.

Sauces
and
Dips

Sauces and Dips

nightshade-free curry powder

Makes about 5 tbsps. (1 serving = 1 tsp)

Ingredients:

- 4 tsps. ground turmeric
- 2 tsps. ground cumin
- 2 tsps. ground coriander
- 2 tsps. dried cilantro
- 2 tsps. ground ginger
- 1 tsp mustard powder
- 1 tsp ground cardamom
- ½ tsp black pepper
- ½ tsp ground cinnamon
- ½ tsp of any of the following:
  - Fenugreek, curry leave, clove, anise, mace, star anise, caraway, nutmeg, garlic powder

Directions:

1. Mix all ingredients together thoroughly.
2. Store in an airtight container at room temperature.

anti-inflammatory spice blend

Ingredients:

- 1 teaspoon turmeric
- 1 teaspoon dry mustard
- 2 tablespoons ground cumin
- 2 tablespoons curry powder
- 2 tablespoons chili powder
- 1 tablespoon ground allspice
- 1 tablespoon black pepper
- 1 teaspoon ground cinnamon

Directions:

1. Mix all ingredients.
2. Store in an airtight container when not using.

healthy ketchup

Ingredients:

- 1 can (6 ounces) tomato paste
- 2 tablespoons apple cider vinegar
- ½ tablespoon Dijon mustard
- ¼ teaspoon cloves
- ¼ teaspoon allspice
- ¼ teaspoon cinnamon
- ½ teaspoon garlic powder
- ½ teaspoon onion powder
- 1 pinch cayenne pepper
- 1 pinch sea salt
- 1 pinch black pepper
- Water, as needed
- Stevia, to taste (optional)

Directions:

1. In a small bowl, combine all ingredients except water and stevia. Whisk together.
2. Add in the water a tablespoon at a time until you reach the consistency you want. Taste as you go and add extra cayenne, sea salt, or pepper as desired. Keep in mind that flavors will continue to blend, and flavors will strengthen as it sits.
3. Place in an airtight container and store in the refrigerator.

olive oil cabernet vinaigrette

Makes 4 servings (1 serving ≈ 1 ½ tablespoons)

Ingredients:

- 1 tablespoon red wine (Cabernet Sauvignon or Merlot)
- 2 tablespoons red wine vinegar
- 1 tablespoon orange juice
- 1 teaspoon fresh garlic, minced
- ½ teaspoon dried basil
- 1 pinch sea salt
- 1 pinch black pepper
- 2 tablespoons extra virgin olive oil

Directions:

1. In a small bowl, whisk together all ingredients except olive oil.
2. Slowly drizzle in olive oil, while whisking, to emulsify the dressing.
3. Serve over mixed greens.

Tips: This recipe can be made ahead and stored in the refrigerator for up to 2 weeks. If chilled, olive may thicken, so allow to come to room temperature before serving.

balsamic mustard vinaigrette

Makes 10 servings (1 serving ≈ 2 tablespoons)

Ingredients:

- ¼ cup balsamic vinegar
- ¼ cup water
- 1 teaspoon Dijon mustard
- Herbs to taste*
- 1 pinch sea salt
- 1 pinch black pepper
- 1 clove garlic, minced
- ⅓ cup cold-pressed, extra-virgin olive oil
- ⅓ cup flaxseed oil (or use all olive oil)
- *Use dried rosemary, oregano, basil, parsley, tarragon, or any herb of choice

Directions:

1. Measure all ingredients, except oils, into a jar with a tight-fitting lid. Shake vigorously or use a whisk. When well-combined, add oils and shake again. Store in refrigerator.
2. Mixture will harden while refrigerated. Remove, and allow to soften 5-10 minutes before using.
3. Use this dressing for any salad or any veggie you wish. You may double the recipe to keep some at your workplace for a quick salad dressing. Remember to store in refrigerator.

Tips: Yields 1 ¼ cup dressing (20 tablespoons).

guacamole

Makes 4 servings

Ingredients:

- 2 cloves garlic, minced (≈ 2 teaspoons)
- 3 scallions or red onion, minced (≈ ¼ cup)
- ¼ jalapeno, minced
- 2 avocados, peeled
- 1 tablespoon fresh lime juice (juice of ½ a lime)
- 2 tablespoons chopped fresh cilantro
- 1 pinch of sea salt

Directions:

1. In a medium bowl, combine the garlic, scallions, and jalapenos.
2. Add avocado and mash using the back of a fork.
3. Gently stir in lime juice.
4. Finish with cilantro and sea salt.

roasted beet hummus

Makes 8 servings (1 serving ≈ ⅓ cup)

Ingredients:

- 2 medium to large roasted beets
- 1 can (15 ounces) chickpeas, drained, rinsed
- ¼ cup tahini
- ¼ cup fresh lemon juice
- 3 tablespoons extra-virgin olive oil
- 3 cloves garlic
- 1 ½ teaspoons sea salt

Directions:

1. Roast beets:
2. Preheat oven to 400 degrees F.
3. Scrub beets with a vegetable brush under running water. Cut off top and bottom.
4. Wrap beets in foil and roast until tender (about 1 hour). Let cool, then peel.
5. Add all ingredients to a blender or food processor. Puree until smooth.

Tips: For a variation, in place of cumin, add ½ to 1 tsp of dried basil or 1-2 tbsps fresh basil.

sweet potato hummus

Makes 8 servings (1 serving ≈ ⅓ cup)

Ingredients:

- 1 large sweet potato (12-14 ounces), cooked and mashed
- 1 can (15 ounces) chickpeas, drained, rinsed
- ¼ cup tahini
- ¼ cup fresh lemon juice
- 3 tablespoons extra-virgin olive oil
- 1 small clove garlic, halved
- 1 ½ teaspoons fine sea salt
- 1 teaspoon ground cumin
- ½ teaspoon cinnamon (optional)

Directions:

1. Add all ingredients to a blender or food processor. Puree until smooth.

Tips: Serve with vegetables or seed crackers. To reduce sodium content perserving, cut added sea salt to half of current amount, add some pepper, or increase the other spices to desired taste.

nut hummus

Makes 7 servings (1 serving = ⅓ cup)

Ingredients:

- 1 cup raw nuts, soaked for 12 hours and rinsed
- ⅔ cup tahini
- ½ cup extra-virgin olive oil
- 3-4 cloves garlic
- Juice 2 small lemons (= 4-6 tbsps)
- ½ tsp sea salt
- ½ tsp black pepper
- ¼ cup sun-dried tomatoes
- ¼ cup chopped fresh parsley
- ½ to 1 small diced habanero or jalapeno pepper to taste (optional)

Directions:

1. Combine all the ingredients in a food processor and puree until smooth.
2. Let the hummus mixture sit in the refrigerator for a couple of hours before serving to let the flavors blend.

Tips: Almonds work best but cashews or other nuts are worth trying for variety and personal preference. This nut hummus is perfect for low carb/paleo type meal plans and serves as a nice dip for raw veggies or seed only crackers.

beet edamame hummus

Makes 4 servings

Ingredients:

- 1 medium to large roasted beet
- 8 oz frozen organic, non-GMO edamame, shelled and steamed
- 2 tbsps. tahini
- 2 tbsps. fresh lemon juice
- 1 ½ tbsp extra-virgin olive oil
- 1 large garlic clove
- ½ tsp sea salt
- Optional: chickpeas, rinsed and dried, parsley

Directions:

1. Preheat oven to 400 degrees F.
2. Scrub the beet with a vegetable brush under running water. Cut off the top and bottom.
3. Wrap the beet in foil and roast until tender (about 1 hour).
4. Let cool, then peel.
5. Place all ingredients in a blender or food processor. Puree until smooth.
6. Optional: Top with parsley and chickpeas

Tips: Use leftover roasted beets to shorten the preparation process.

dairy-free pesto

Makes 1 cup (approximately 8 servings; 1 serving = 2 tbsps.)

Ingredients:

- ⅓ cup pine nuts
- 1 ½ cup packed basil leaves
- 3 cloves garlic
- 1 ½ tsps. fresh lemon juice
- ½ tsps. sea salt
- ⅓ cup extra-virgin olive oil

Directions:

1. Lightly toast the pine nuts in a skillet over low heat for 5 mins. Shake the pan from time to time to make sure the pine nuts don't burn.
2. Place all the remaining ingredients except the oil in a small food processor. Pulse a few times to chop the contents.
3. With blender or food processor on low speed, slowly drizzle in the olive oil until a paste has formed. Continue blending for 15 seconds until the sauce has a smooth and creamy texture.

Tips: If not using right away, pour into ice cube trays, cover with a thin layer of olive oil, and freeze. Once frozen, remove from trays and keep in glass containers in the freezer for later use.

Snacks

Snacks

savory seed crackers

Makes 8 servings (1 serving ≈ one 2-inch by 3-inch cracker or two 1-inch by 1.5-inch crackers)

Ingredients:

- ⅓ cup chia seeds
- ⅓ cup flax seeds
- ⅓ cup sunflower seeds
- ¼ cup water
- ⅛ teaspoon garlic powder
- ⅛ teaspoon onion powder
- ¼ teaspoon salt
- ¼ teaspoon guar or xanthan gum
- More water, if needed

Directions:

1. Preheat oven to 300 degrees F.
2. Mix all ingredients together and spread on greased parchment paper on a cookie sheet. Press flat (about ⅛-inch thick).
3. Bake for about 30 minutes on each side.
4. Immediately after removal from oven, score the seeds (they will still be pliable at this point, but score right away, as they will firm up quickly). A pizza cutter works well.

Tips: Before spreading on cookie sheet, oil hands or spatula, to keep seeds from sticking to hands.. May consider longer duration of time at lower cooking temperature (i.e., 250°F).

marinated olives

Makes 6 servings (1 serving ≈ ⅓ cup olives)

Ingredients:

- 2 cups olives (mixed varieties, large, small, multi-colored)
- 2 tablespoons olive oil
- 6 thin slices of lemon peel
- 6 thin slices of orange peel
- 2 cloves garlic, slivered
- 1 teaspoon fresh lemon juice
- ¼ teaspoon orange zest
- ¼ teaspoon lemon zest
- ¼ teaspoon whole coriander seeds
- 1 bay leaf

Directions:

1. Combine all ingredients together in an air-tight container (such as a glass storage dish or large jar), and place in the refrigerator.
2. Allow to marinate for at least 2 days and stir occasionally.

gluten-free baking powder biscuits

Makes 12 servings (1 serving = 1 biscuit)

Ingredients:

- 1 ½ cup brown rice flour
- ½ cup tapioca flour
- 4 teaspoons baking powder
- ⅛ teaspoon salt
- 3 tablespoons coconut oil
- 1 cup unsweetened applesauce

Directions:

1. Preheat oven to 425 degrees F.
2. In a medium-large mixing bowl, stir together dry ingredients (brown rice flour, tapioca flour, baking powder, and salt).
3. Sprinkle oil on top, and mix well with a pastry blender or fork, until consistency is crumbly.
4. Mix in applesauce and stir until blended.
5. Drop 12 equal spoonfuls onto an ungreased cookie sheet. With spoon, lightly shape into biscuit.
6. Bake 15-18 minutes until slightly browned.

Tips: Serve warm for best flavor but may be lightly reheated in a microwave.

cashew-dusted kale chips

Makes 16 servings (1 serving = ⅓ cup)

Ingredients:

- 2 lbs kale
- ¼ cup coconut oil
- 1 tbsp lemon juice (optional)
- ½ tsp sea salt
- ⅓ cup raw cashews, ground
- 1 tbsp nutritional yeast

Directions:

1. Preheat oven to 350 degrees F (if baking in oven and not in a dehydrator).
2. Strip the kale from the tough stems. Rinse thoroughly and dry. Tear or chop into smaller pieces and set aside.
3. Make a dressing in a large bowl with the coconut oil, lemon juice, and salt. Toss with kale to coat. Massage for about 1 min to break down vegetable fibers.
4. Sprinkle kale with ground nuts and nutritional yeast. Toss again.
5. Place kale in a single layer on dehydrator sheets or baking pans. Single layers provide the best results from dehydrating or baking. If kale is piled in more than one layer it will steam and not get crispy.
6. Dehydrate for 2 hours or according to dehydrator directions for greens. If baking in oven, bake for 15 mins until leaves are crispy and crunchy. Cool completely before serving or storing in an airtight container.

Tips: These kale chips turn out best in a dehydrator. Watch closely if baking in oven, as kale can burn easily.

seaweed snacks

Makes 2 servings

Ingredients:

- 4 sheets of toasted nori
- 2 tbsps. olive oil (not extra virgin)
- Spice options: sea salt, wasabi powder, sriracha, or garlic powder

Directions:

1. Preheat oven to 250 degrees F.
2. Cut nori into small squares or large strips using sharp scissors.
3. In a very small mixing bowl (like a ramekin), mix oil with spice of choice and/or salt. Spread oil with spices evenly over nori sheets (use a pastry brush or the back of a spoon).
4. Place nori sheets on oiled baking sheet. Bake for 15-20 mins. Let cool and store in an airtight container.

Tips: For a variation, use pickled ginger juice instead of oil and spices.

chewy crunchy road mix

Makes 4-6 servings

Ingredients:

- ½ cup walnuts or pecans
- ¼ cup almonds
- 1/4 cup pistachios
- 1/2 dried apricots
- 1/2 cup dates
- 1/2 cup figs

Directions:

1. Mix all ingredients together. Divide recipe into four servings and store in small containers to take with you for an on-the-go snack.
2. Free or refrigerate to preserve freshness if not planning to use right away.

Tips: May use different nuts and seeds as desired.

crispy Brussels sprouts chips

Makes 4 servings

Ingredients:

- 2 lbs. Brussels sprouts, washed and dried
- 2 tbsps organic coconut oil, melted
- ¼ tsp sea salt
- ¼ tsp pepper
- Lemon zest (optional)

Directions:

1. Preheat oven to 300 degrees F.
2. Cut the bottom tip off each Brussels sprout. Trim any damaged outer leaves from the sprouts, then separate all of the remaining leave.
3. Place the sprout leaves in a large bowl. Mix with the coconut oil, salt, pepper, and lemon zest.
4. Divide the sprouts between two large baking trays. Spread evenly in a single layer for best results.
5. Bake for 8-10 mins or until sprouts are crispy and brown around the edges.
6. Let cool and serve. May be kept in an airtight container for a few days.

raspberry chia seed pudding

Makes 4 servings

Ingredients:

- 2 cups organic raspberries, divided
- ¾ cup full-fat coconut milk
- ¼ tsp sea salt
- ½ tsp real vanilla extract
- ½ tsp cinnamon
- ½ cup chia seeds
- ½ cup dried coconut flakes (unsweetened)
- 2 tbsps. hemp seeds
- ¼ cup raw walnuts, finely chopped

Directions:

1. In a blender, puree 1 cup of raspberries with coconut milk until smooth.
2. Place salt, vanilla, cinnamon, and chia seeds in a bowl. Pour the raspberry mixture into the bowl and stir to combine. Seal in an airtight container in the refrigerator for 12 hours or overnight. This mixture will become thicker and pudding-like.
3. When ready, give mixture a stir. Divide into four small bowls and top with coconut, hemp seeds, walnuts, and remaining berries.

roasted rosemary almonds

Makes 16 servings (1 serving = 2 tbsp)

Ingredients:

- 1 tbsp unrefined coconut oil
- 2 cups raw whole almonds
- 2 tbsps. dried rosemary
- 2 tsps. sea salt
- ¼ tsp black pepper

Directions:

1. Put coconut oil in a large skillet over medium-low heat.
2. Add in the almonds and stir until well coated. Add the rosemary, salt, and pepper.
3. Toast the almonds in the skillet for about 8 to 12 mins. Stir often to avoid burning. Transfer the nuts to a plate and cool to room temperature.

dehydrated kale chips

Makes 12 servings (1 serving ≈ ½ cup)

Ingredients:

- 2 bunches kale (Dino or curly varieties)
- ¼ cup olive oil
- ¼ teaspoon sea salt

Directions:

1. Rinse kale and pat dry. Cut away kale from large main veins and chop into 2-inch pieces.
2. Place chopped kale into a mixing bowl. Pour ¼ cup of olive oil over the chopped kale and toss well to coat. Massage the olive oil and salt into the kale for about 3 minutes. (Can put it in a plastic bag and shake it up first.)
3. Place kale evenly over dehydrator trays. Close the dehydrator and turn on.
4. Dehydrate for 2 hours at 145° F

dehydrated sweet potato chips

Makes 3 servings

Ingredients:

- 1 large sweet potato
- 1 teaspoon olive oil
- ¼ teaspoon sea salt

Directions:

1. Slice the sweet potato thinly. If you have an adjustable mandolin slicer, put it on the thin setting (0.5 mm) and use the hand guard. Put the slices into a large bowl.
2. Drizzle the sweet potato slices with olive oil and sprinkle with sea salt until well covered.
3. Dehydrate the chips in the dehydrator on at least 115° F for 24 hours or until crispy.

Tip: Chips start to get soft soon after they are taken out of the dehydrator so put them in an airtight container and consume within a few days.

dehydrated sweet potato chips with cinnamon

Makes 3 servings

Ingredients:

- 1 large sweet potato
- 1 cup orange juice
- 1 tablespoon agave
- 1 teaspoon molasses
- 1 teaspoon cinnamon
- 2 tablespoons olive oil

Directions:

1. Slice the sweet potato thinly. If you have an adjustable mandolin slicer, put it on the thin setting (0.5 mm) and use the hand guard. Put slices into a large bowl.
2. Blend remaining ingredients in a blender. Pour this solution over potatoes and mix thoroughly. Allow potato slices to soak in the solution for about 15 minutes to absorb flavors.
3. Place in a preheated 350° oven on a cookie sheet or glass 9x13 casserole. Bake for 10 minutes or until crisp yet tender. You can skip this step and go directly to step 4.
4. Spread on dehydrator trays and dehydrate on at least 115° F for 24 hours or until crispy

roasted sweet potato fries

Makes 6 servings (1 serving ≈ ¾ cup)

Ingredients:

- 5 medium sweet potatoes, cut into about 1 by 5-inch strips
- 3 tablespoons olive oil
- 2 tablespoons finely chopped fresh basil leaves
- 2 teaspoons kosher salt
- ½ teaspoon freshly ground black pepper

Directions:

1. Preheat oven to 400° F.
2. Place the sweet potato strips on a baking sheet lined with foil. Drizzle with olive oil. Spread potatoes out in pan, so that they are in a single layer. Bake until golden, about 45 minutes.
3. While potatoes are baking, combine the basil, salt, and pepper in a small bowl. Stir to mix.
4. When the sweet potato fries come out of the oven and are still hot, sprinkle with the basil mixture.

spice seed crackers

Makes 8 servings(1 serving ≈ one 2-inch by 3-inch cracker or two 1-inch by 1½-inch crackers)

Ingredients:

- ⅓ cup chia seeds
- ⅓ cup flax seeds
- ⅓ cup sunflower seeds
- ¼ cup agave (natural sweetener, or combo)
- ¼ teaspoon allspice or cinnamon
- 1 teaspoon vanilla extract
- ¼ teaspoon guar or xanthan gum
- 2–4 tablespoons water, if needed

Directions:

1. Preheat oven to 300° F.
2. In a medium bowl, mix all ingredients together. Spread on greased parchment paper on a cookie sheet. Press flat (about an ⅛-inch thick).
3. Bake for about 30 minutes on each side.
4. Immediately after removal from oven, score the seed crackers to make 8 servings (they will still be pliable at this point, but score right away, as they will harden quickly). A pizza cutter works well.

Tips: Before spreading on cookie sheet, put oil on hands or spatula, to keep seeds from sticking to hands. Watch closely so that you don't burn the seeds. Can cook for longer at a lower temperature (i.e., 250° F).

chia seed applesauce bread

Makes 16 servings (1 serving ≈ one 2 ¼-inch by 2 ¼ -inch square)

Ingredients:

- 1 cup teff flour
- 1 cup rice flour
- 3 tablespoons chia seed
- 1 teaspoon baking soda
- ½ teaspoon cinnamon
- ¼ teaspoon salt
- ¼ teaspoon nutmeg
- 1 cup unsweetened applesauce
- 1 tablespoon coconut oil, melted
- ½ cup brown rice syrup
- 3 ½ tablespoons apple butter
- 1 teaspoon pure vanilla extract
- 1 large apple, peeled, cored, and chopped

Egg replacer:

- ⅓ cup water
- 1 tablespoon ground flax seed

Directions:

1. Prepare the egg replacer by mixing the ground flax and water. Allow to sit for 5 minutes to gel.
2. In a large bowl, mix dry ingredients (teff and rice flours, chia seed, baking soda, cinnamon, salt, and nutmeg). In a smaller bowl, mix wet ingredients (applesauce, melted coconut oil, brown rice syrup, apple butter and vanilla extract).
3. Add the wet ingredients to the dry ingredients. Stir in apple chunks.
4. Pour mixture into oiled 9-inch square pan.
5. Bake at 350 degrees F for 30 minutes.
6. When cooled, cut into 16 servings.

Tips: Alternatives include oat flour in place of rice flour, and natural sweetener, agave nectar, or fruit juice concentrate in place of brown rice syrup.

Desserts

Desserts

crispy rice squares

Makes 32 squares (1 serving ≈ one 2-inch by 2-inch square)

Ingredients:

- 1 teaspoon cold-pressed coconut oil
- ½ cup brown rice syrup
- 2 tablespoon almond butter
- 3 teaspoon vanilla extract
- 2 cups crispy brown rice cereal
- 2 cups puffed rice
- 2 cups puffed millet
- ½ cup pumpkin seeds or sunflower seeds
- ½ cup currants, chopped dried apples or dates

Directions:

1. Heat oil in a large pot. Add rice syrup and almond butter. Stir until bubbly.
2. Remove from heat and stir in vanilla.
3. Add remaining ingredients and mix well with a wooden spoon.
4. Press into an ungreased 9 x 13-inch pan and press mixture flat. Let mixture set at room temperature or refrigerate.
5. Cut into squares. Store in an airtight container.

Tips: Substitutions: agave syrup for brown rice syrup; tahini for almond butter, currents or dates for dried apples, and grape seed oil for coconut oil.

fresh berries with coconut mango cream

Makes 4 servings

Ingredients:

- ⅔ cups coconut milk (canned)
- 1 ⅓ cups diced frozen mango (do not defrost)
- 1 teaspoon vanilla
- 2 cups fresh blueberries, blackberries, cranberries, or raspberries

Garnish:

- **Optional toppings:** 4 mint leaves, chia seeds, or roasted coconut flakes

Directions:

1. To a blender, add coconut milk and frozen mango. Blend on high until smooth.
2. Add vanilla and blend again for several seconds.
3. Evenly divide berries among four dishes. Top with coconut cream.
4. Garnish with a mint leaf, if desired.

Tips: For a variation, add ⅓ cup frozen raspberries to coconut milk and mango (step 1). The pink color is beautiful on top of the berries.

lemon cream with blackberries and raspberries

Makes 4 servings

Ingredients:

- 1 tablespoon grated lemon zest, divided
- ¼ cup fresh lemon juice
- 1/4 cup maple or agave syrup
- 1 package (12 ounces) silken tofu, firm, or extra-firm, drained
- ½ cup fresh blackberries
- ½ cup fresh raspberries

Directions:

1. Combine 2 ½ teaspoons of the lemon zest, lemon juice, syrup, and tofu in a blender or food processor. Puree ingredients until smooth, scraping down sides of blender with a rubber spatula as necessary.
2. Divide lemon cream evenly among four bowls or serving glasses. Garnish each portion with berries and reserve ½ teaspoon of lemon zest.
3. Serve immediately or refrigerate.

Tips: You can make the lemon cream in advance, cover it, and keep it in the refrigerator for three days.

coconut chocolate truffles

Makes 30 truffles (1 serving = 2 truffles)

Ingredients:

- ½ cup full fat canned unsweetened coconut milk
- 1 tsp almond, orange, vanilla, or hazelnut extract
- 8 oz bittersweet dark chocolate (at least 70% cocoa), finely chopped
- ¼ cup cocoa powder or chopped nuts for coating

Directions:

1. In a small saucepan, bring the coconut milk to a simmer. Stir in the extract, then pour the mixture over the chocolate in a separate bowl. Let stand a few mins before stirring until smooth. Allow to cool, then refrigerate for 30 mins to 1 hour. (Remove mixture from the refrigerator while it is still malleable).
2. Using a small spoon, form 1-inch balls and roll them quickly between your palms. Place balls on a baking sheet lined with parchment paper. Refrigerate overnight.
3. Roll in cocoa powder or chopped nuts. Store the truffles in an airtight container in the refrigerator for up to a week.

fresh berries with coconut raspberry cream

Makes 4 servings

Ingredients:
- ⅔ cup full-fat coconut milk
- 1 ⅓ cup frozen organic raspberries (do not defrost)
- 1 tsp vanilla
- 2 cups fresh organic raspberries, blueberries or blackberries, washed, rinsed, and dried

Garnish:
- 2 mint leaves per serving (optional)

Directions:

1. Place coconut milk and frozen raspberries in a blender. Blend on high until smooth.
2. Add vanilla and blend again for several seconds.
3. Divide fresh berries among four dishes and top with coconut cream.
4. Garnish with mint leaves, if desired.

chocolate protein ice cream

Makes 4 servings

Ingredients:

- 2 cups sliced bananas
- 2 tsp cocoa powder
- 1 cup chocolate protein powder
- 1 tsp vanilla extract
- 1 cup unsweetened almond milk
- Optional: cacao nibs

Directions:

1. Place ingredients in a food processor- Immediately place frozen bananas into the food processor when you remove them from the freezer (the ice cream won't work if the bananas aren't frozen). Add the cocoa powder, protein powder, almond milk, and vanilla.
2. Blend until smooth- Cover the food processor and blend until smooth. You may need to scrape the sides a couple of times.
3. Add more almond milk- If the protein nice cream isn't blending well, add another teaspoon or two to the food processor and blend until it turns into a soft serve consistency.
4. Serve immediately, top with cacao nibs

chocolate pumpkin bread

Makes 4 servings

Ingredients:

- egg replacer (⅓ cup water mixed with 1 tablespoon ground flax seed)
- 1 cup pumpkin puree
- 1 cup almond milk
- 2 tsp vanilla
- 1 tsp natural sweetener
- 1 cup coconut oil
- 1 tsp coconut sugar
- 1 cup cocoa powder
- Optional: pecans or walnuts

Directions:

1. Prepare the egg replacer by mixing the ground flax and water. Allow to sit for 5 minutes to gel. Mix all of the wet ingredients in a separate bowl until combined. Set aside.
2. Add dry ingredients to the wet ingredients. Add the dry ingredients to a separate bowl and whisk them together.
3. Add all the ingredients together. Slowly add the dry to the wet ingredients
4. Don't forget the coconut oil. Last but not least add the melted coconut oil right before adding the bread batter to the loaf pan.
5. Pour the batter into the loaf pan. Spray a loaf pan with non stick cooking spray and pour the bread batter into the loaf pan.
6. Bake. Place the bread into the oven and bake for 45-50 minutes. You may need to add a tin foil tent around 30 minutes depending on your oven.
7. Let the bread rest. Remove the bread from the oven and let it sit in the pan for 10 minutes. Slide a knife along the bread and the loaf pan to loosen the bread and then remove the bread from the pan.

About the Author

Dr. Rani (Rudrani) Banik is a board-certified ophthalmologist, fellowship-trained neuro-ophthalmologist, and certified functional medicine practitioner.

Dr. Banik offers the best traditional management of ophthalmic disease, combined with an integrative approach. Her treatment protocols promote eye and brain health based on nutrition, botanicals, lifestyle modification, movement, essential oils, and supplements.

Dr. Banik is the founder of EnVision Health, a private practice in New York City. Dr. Banik is an Associate Professor of Ophthalmology at Mount Sinai's Icahn School of Medicine, where she is involved in clinical trials research and teaching. She has authored numerous articles and has presented at national and international meetings. She is a Castle Connolly Top Doctor and New York Magazine Best Doctor.

Dr. Banik's mission is to educate the public and her colleagues about eye-smart nutrition and lifestyle choices to prevent vision loss and achieve better overall health and quality of life.

Dr. Banik is often featured as an eye health expert in the media; she has been interviewed by the New York Times, Good Morning America, CBS, NBC, ABC, and many other television and radio programs. She has been an expert guest on over 75 podcasts.

"Dr. Rani's Visionary Kitchen" is the companion cookbook to "Beyond Carrots," Dr. Banik's first book. Her next book, "Beyond Leafy Greens - 7 Integrative Strategies to Fight Macular Degeneration," will be released soon. Be sure to connect with Dr. Banik on social media via her Facebook group, EnVision Health, or on Instagram at @dr.ranibanik for valuable tips on protecting and preserving your vision.

Made in the USA
Monee, IL
26 June 2025

20011846R10085